MORE THAN PETTICOATS

REMARKABLE
CONNECTICUT
WOMEN

MORE THAN PETTICOATS

REMARKABLE CONNECTICUT WOMEN

Antonia Petrash

TWODOT®

GUILFORD, CONNECTICUT
HELENA, MONTANA
AN IMPRINT OF THE GLOBE PEQUOT PRESS

A · TWODOT® · BOOK

Cover photo: Ladies Cycle Club of Hartford, courtesy of The Connecticut Historical Society, Hartford, Connecticut

Library of Congress Cataloging-in-Publication Data

Petrash, Antonia.
    More than petticoats : remarkable Connecticut women / Antonia Petrash.— 1st ed.
    p. cm. — (More than petticoats series)
    Includes bibliographical references and index.
    Contents: Anna Warner Bailey — Julia Evelina Smith and Abby Hadassah Smith — Prudence Crandall — Harriet Beecher Stowe — Caroline Maria Hewins — Martha Minerva Franklin — Mary Jobe Akeley — Katharine Houghton Hepburn — Sophie Tucker — Eva Lutz Butler — Margaret Fogarty Rudkin — Gladys Tantaquidgeon.
    ISBN 0-7627-2371-8
    I. Women—Connecticut—Biography. 2. Women—Connecticut—History. 3. Connecticut—Biography. I. Title: Remarkable Connecticut women. II. Title. III. Series.

    CT3262.C66P48 2003
    920.72'09746—dc22
[B]
                                                          2003056369

Manufactured in the United States of America
First Edition/First Printing

Contents

ᴀCKNOWLEDGMENTS

A work that depends on such intense research also depends heavily on the help of others—librarians, historians, and archivists who spend much of their lives often thanklessly documenting and preserving the past for researchers to explore, enjoy, and write about. I am indebted to a host of such generous professionals throughout the State of Connecticut who offered assistance in checking facts and in obtaining photos and documents. Although I cannot mention them all, special thanks should go to Janice Mathews, Curator of the Hartford Collection at the Hartford Public Library; Sabra Ionno of the Harriet Beecher Stowe Center; Nancy Finlay of the Connecticut Historical Society; Dorrie Hanna and archivists at the Mystic River Historical Society; Beatrice Thomson of the Anna Warner Bailey Chapter of the Daughters of the American Revolution; Melissa Tantaquidgeon and Sandy Dufresne of the Mohegan Nation; Jeremy McGraw of the Billy Rose Theatre Collection, the New York Public Library; Nan Redmond of Pepperidge Farm; George Sherman of Campbell Soup Co.; and Danita Bowen and Lisa Lopez of the Dixwell Community House in New Haven.

Phyllis Reed and James F. Bennett of the Glastonbury Historical Society offered invaluable assistance in my research of the colorful Smith sisters. Jackie Zeppieri and David Butler were most generous with information about Eva Lutz Butler and permission to use Butler family letters. Sincere appreciation goes to Joan Cohn of The Indian & Colonial Research Center in Old Mystic for providing not only help in researching the lives of Eva Lutz Butler and Gladys Tantaquidgeon, but the generous hand of friendship.

Special thanks to my editors Charlene Patterson and Shelley Wolf for their emotional support and their practical recommendations throughout the many months of the project. Last, I am especially enriched by and indebted to my own personal circle of inspiration—my co-workers at the Glen Cove Public Library, my supportive friends, my sisters and their families, my wonderfully encouraging daughters and sons-in-law and grandsons, and my husband, Jack, whose steadfast support and encouragement helps me turn my dreams into realities.

$\mathcal{I}$NTRODUCTION

$\mathcal{I}$f size alone was the deciding factor in a state's ability to produce remarkable women then, by rights, Connecticut should have come up short. The third smallest state in the United States, it covers only about 5,000 square miles; in the year 2000 its population numbered only about three and a half million people. In contrast, its neighbor New York boasts more than ten times its area, with a population of about nineteen million people.

But studying the lives of the women chronicled here has proven that, without a doubt, size is irrelevant—the state they lived in may have been small but their achievements were not. Connecticut's remarkable women founded economic dynasties, played a pivotal role in the abolition of slavery, preserved a Native American nation, and helped secure equal rights for all members of society. They scaled forbidding mountain ranges, challenged preconceived notions of who could be a successful entertainer, and even changed a nation's eating habits. They rejected many of the limits imposed on them, broke rules they felt were unfair, and made their own.

By rights, these women should have been an ineffectual, powerless group. All were born before 1900, into a society where women's political and economic rights were severely restricted, a society where most women's destinies were pre-ordained. While men were generally free to choose their vocations in life and were encouraged to develop their individual potential and to explore the world around them, women enjoyed few such freedoms. Instead they were encouraged by society to keep to the traditional "women's sphere," caring for home, husband, and family.

Working women's vocational choices were limited to teaching

and, later, nursing or perhaps factory work. Even the renowned world explorer Mary Jobe Akeley began her professional life as a teacher. If a woman chose to marry, as most women did, any dreams of a career she might have were often cut short by the responsibilities of a large family, poor health care, or laws that gave her husband total control over her property and finances.

The brave women who chafed at these restrictions and who tried to chart their own course as their fathers and brothers did saw their personal power severely limited, not only by societal disapproval but by restricted access to a tool those fathers and brothers took for granted—an education. Education was often thought to be a wasteful luxury that should not be squandered on mere girls and women. Although girls might be given a rudimentary education at a local school or be taught music and embroidery arts at a boarding school, those born in the eighteenth and early nineteenth centuries were denied access to higher education, as no colleges would accept them. Black women's opportunities were even more limited. Prudence Crandall was jailed in 1833 for daring to open a school for young black girls in Canterbury.

Those who were fortunate enough to be born later in the nineteenth century enjoyed some opportunities previously denied their sex. By the end of that century more women were attending college and entering professions previously closed to them. With the passage of the Nineteenth Amendment in 1920, women could finally vote and could finally begin the long, arduous climb to achieving a modicum of equal rights with men. But even in 1899, when the last of the thirteen women portrayed in this book was born, most women were still hobbled by a lack of any real political or economic power.

But these remarkable women from Connecticut were different from most. When power proved elusive, they fought for it. When power was denied them, they created their own, eventually emerging as leaders who plotted their own destinies and who helped others to do the same.

The Smith sisters of Glastonbury, two elderly ladies past the time in their lives when society deemed them useful, showed just how useful they could be by vigorously protesting what they considered to be the unfair practice of taxing women who, of course, could not vote. Their protests encouraged others to take up the cause for suffrage, and their voices still resonate through their writings, reminding us that the responsibility to fight for freedom and equal rights is a duty borne by all of a nation's citizens—young and old.

Harriet Beecher Stowe's father mourned the fact that she had been born a girl and thus would never be able to influence society by speaking in public as her brothers could. So she picked up her pen and wrote a story so powerful that it is said to have been a major cause of the Civil War and one of the major influences in the success of the abolition movement.

Eva Lutz Butler and Gladys Tantaquidgeon both worked from their villages near Mystic to preserve the heritage of the Native American. As all the women labored and fought their own individual battles, their work, and ultimately their achievements, wove an invisible web of support that other women could build upon, a web that would spin on into the future for other young women to grasp.

One of the problems faced in the writing of this book was limiting the number of women to be included in the volume. So many more deserve to have their wonderful stories heard, but because of space limitations they do not appear within these pages. For instance, Hannah Bunce Watson took over the publication of the *Hartford Courant* when the publisher, her husband Ebenezer Watson, died in 1777; she thus became one of the first women publishers in the new land. Sarah Pierce defied public opinion that frowned on education for girls and opened one of the first schools for young women in 1792 in Litchfield; Sarah Porter followed her lead and established Miss Porter's School in 1841 in Farmington. Charlotte Perkins Gilman was a prolific lecturer and writer of feminist papers who, in 1898, shocked society by calling for the establishment of day care centers to promote the economic independence of women. Mabel Osgood Wright was a pioneer in environmental education who founded the Connecticut Audubon Society in 1896 and opened one of the first bird sanctuaries in the nation in Fairfield in 1914. Marian Anderson, a world-renowned operatic contralto, fought against racial bias to become the first black singer to perform at the Metropolitan Opera in New York City in 1955. And although born just after 1900, out of this book's time range, it is difficult to ignore the accomplishments of Clare Booth Luce, who became the first U. S. congresswoman from Connecticut in 1941, and Ella Grasso, who in 1974 was the first woman elected governor of a state in her own right.

Connecticut is sometimes known as the "Land of Steady Habits," supposedly because of the strict morals of its inhabitants. Apparently one of its "steady habits" is producing remarkable women who have literally changed not just their small state but their world for the better.

ANNA WARNER BAILEY
1758–1851

The Heroine of Groton

*A*n eerie silence fell over the coastal village of Groton. Although it was a bright summer day, the stores and homes were deserted, the streets strangely empty and still. The people had gathered their children and what household belongings they could carry and had fled inland in fear of their very lives. The British were coming, it was rumored, coming to Groton once again, coming to crush the efforts of the American Commodore Stephen Decatur, captain of two frigates and a sloop of war that were barricaded up the Thames River. The people of Groton knew the British well. The British had struck their town once before—during the Revolutionary War—and although it had been more than thirty years since that attack, old and young knew only too well what horror they could wreak. On this summer day in 1813 the villagers were not going to wait around for it to happen again.

A young American soldier trudged wearily through the empty streets, wondering absently where all the people had gone, but more importantly how he was to fulfill his important mission from his commanding officer. "Gather up all the flannel you can," Major

Anna Warner Bailey

Simeon Smith had ordered. Flannel was used as wadding for cartridges for the guns on which the village militia depended for its protection. But where was he to find such wadding, with all the shops shuttered and the houses deserted? And how would he explain his dereliction of duty to his harried and besieged major?

Suddenly he spied in the distance an elderly lady crossing the main street, and he hurried up to her and explained his dilemma. Did she know where he could find the flannel the war effort so desperately needed?

Anna Warner Bailey had lived through the siege of Fort Griswold by the British in September 1781. She had seen how the enemy had slaughtered her relatives and friends. Now that same enemy might return to threaten her home and family once again. She was not shy about voicing her hatred toward them. But imagine the young soldier's surprise when the lady suddenly reached beneath her skirts, pulled off a red flannel petticoat, and handed it to him. "Here," she said, "use this for your wadding, and there are plenty more where that came from."

The young soldier turned and headed back to the fort, carrying the red flannel petticoat triumphantly with him. Anna Warner Bailey's "Martial Petticoat" would forever be a symbol of one woman's patriotism, a woman who lost a petticoat but gained a place in history and in the hearts of her countrymen for bravery and patriotism exhibited during not just one war but two!

Anna Warner was born in Groton, Connecticut, on October 11, 1758. Her father was Philip Warner, a sailor who had moved from Stafford, Connecticut, to New London, Connecticut, to find work in that maritime community. Her mother was Hannah Mills, whose father, John Mills, had originally come from Boston. Anna and her brother were just young children when their mother, Hannah, died of smallpox. A distraught Philip attended to his wife's burial and then set out to sea, only to die himself ten days later from the same disease. The orphaned children were taken in by their maternal grandmother and her husband who lived about 3 miles east of the town of Groton.

Little is written about Anna's childhood and adolescence, though we can surmise she lived as most young girls of the colonial era did, helping with the household tasks of raising and preparing food, making candles and soap, taking care of the animals, and perhaps spinning yarn to make the family clothes. Her education was probably limited to the local school, ending during her teen years when the household tasks began to command more and more of her attention. In addition to her grandparents and brother, two of her uncles, James and Edward Mills, lived in the grandparents' household; Edward was married and the father of two young children.

Women's activities were usually confined to answering the needs of the household, but with the approach of the Revolutionary War those traditional lines between men's and women's domains began to blur. Women struggled to stay informed. Those who could, read the newspapers and pamphlets that circulated throughout their villages. Those with a talent for writing wrote articles and poems for the local newspapers in support of the patriot cause. The Revolution forced even young women such as Anna to develop a greater political awareness, and when the first sounds of battle rang in 1775, their patriotism rivaled that of their husbands, fathers, brothers, and sons. Anna was just sixteen years old when the Revolutionary War began, and it is said she often "wished she were a man" that she might take a more active role in the defense of her new country.

Since British cloth and tea were boycotted, patriotic colonial women were expected to produce homespun cloth and linen to replace British cloth, and to find alternatives to the much-loved British tea. Thus they served their families coffee and herbal tea instead of real tea, and collected money from their neighbors for uniforms and weapons. They tanned goat hides to make the drums that called the soldiers to battle and stuffed gun cartridges for those soldiers to shoot. They ran family farms and businesses when their husbands and fathers were away fighting. And they often played reluctant hosts to enemy troops when the British took over their homes, forcing the women to cook and clean and give comfort to the enemy.

By the summer of 1781 the colonies had been at war for more than six years. Anna Warner and her family lived throughout the war on their small farm near Groton. The surrounding area boasted a strong patriotic fervor and regularly sent out privateer ships from New London to prey on British supply vessels and merchant ships. Such ships, privately owned and armed but licensed by the State of Connecticut, usually enjoyed success in their raids and brought home great wealth for their owners. They also deprived the British of sorely needed stores and highly prized riches.

But sought-after British goods such as salt and sterling were not all the privateers brought home—their daring raids drew the wrath of the British army right home to Groton and New London. To retaliate against these "rebel pirates," the British attacked the area in the summer of 1781. To head the expedition against his own countrymen they chose the infamous traitor, Benedict Arnold.

Benedict Arnold had been born in nearby Norwich, Connecticut, and was familiar with the New London–Groton harbor and its access to the Thames River. He had defected to the British cause in 1780, and as far as the British were concerned he was an excellent choice for the job of attacking his home state. The mouth of the Thames River was defended by Fort Trumbull on the western New London side and Fort Griswold on the eastern Groton side.

The morning of September 6, 1781, dawned in Groton and New London to the sound of cannon fire. Residents rushed to a nearby hill to watch in horror as no fewer than twenty-five British ships landed troops on both sides of the river. Benedict Arnold led the force into New London to burn that city and destroy its storehouses, while Colonel Eyre and Major Montgomery led a contingent of troops on the Groton side, heading for Fort Griswold. Colonel William Ledyard was the American commander charged with defending the fort.

The American troops had devised a method to sound an alarm if just such an attack were to happen: Two cannon shots would call the troops from their homes to defend the fort, three shots were the all clear. When the Americans saw the British troops land, they hastily fired the two shots. But to their horror another shot was fired, mistakenly giving the all clear. It was believed that Benedict Arnold knew the code and had ordered the third shot to deliberately delay the fort's defense.

In the small farmhouse 3 miles distant, Anna's Uncle Edward Mills heard the cannon, and despite the confusion of the call, decided to head for the fort. A corporal in the militia, he felt keenly his duty to defend his family and his young country. Once at the fort he joined others to watch New London burn and to try to defend against the attacking British troops.

The battle of Fort Griswold has been recorded as one of the bloodiest massacres of the Revolutionary War. Although the 150 Americans fought bravely, they were no match for the more than 800 British soldiers who attacked the fort on three sides. Major Montgomery was killed, and despite an attempt at surrender, American Commander Colonel Ledyard was murdered with his own bayonet. When the dust of battle settled, eighty-eight American soldiers were dead. The wounded and dying were carried to Ebenezer Avery's house nearby.

Throughout that long day, as they cared for the children and milked the cows, Anna and her family waited for news of Edward.

They had heard the ominous sound of the cannons in the early morning and had watched the dark plumes of smoke rising in the distance throughout the day. As evening fell they received news from passersby that both New London and Groton had been burned, Fort Griswold taken, and the casualties were high. After a sleepless night Anna could wait no longer. She arose early the next morning and started off on foot for the village to find news of her uncle.

On the main road to Groton she met many others on the same somber errand—wives seeking news of their husbands, mothers searching frantically for their sons, members of the militia anxiously hurrying toward the coastal village to join their units and lend assistance. When she finally reached the village she received news that her uncle was seriously wounded and had been taken to the makeshift hospital at the Avery house.

She found him, stretched on the floor, bleeding profusely, suffering in pain from both his grievous wounds and his severe anxiety for his family. "Please," he begged Anna, "please bring my family here to me." He feared he would never see them again.

Shocked by the extent of his injuries, Anna did not stop to consider her fatigue, but turned immediately and walked the 3 miles back to the farm. They must move quickly, she told her startled aunt upon her return. There was no time to lose. Running out to the field she caught and saddled the family horse, helped her aunt mount, and placed the oldest child on the distraught woman's lap. Slinging the baby on her hip, Anna led the way through the war-torn countryside to where her uncle lay dying. There in the modest farmhouse the small family was reunited for a last, poignant farewell. Edward Mills died soon after.

On October 19, 1781, British General Lord Charles Cornwallis surrendered to American General George Washington at Yorktown. The Revolution officially ended with the signing of a peace treaty on September 3, 1783. Peace came to the village of

Groton, and Anna and her family put their anger at the British behind them and began their new life as citizens of a new country.

After the war Anna married Elijah Bailey, who became postmaster of the town and served in that capacity for more than forty years. The towns of Groton and nearby Mystic began to flourish once again as the shipbuilding trade was revived and sloops and fishing smacks once again sailed out of the harbor. The industry profited handsomely from the conflict between Britain and France that began in 1793. The United States, declaring neutrality, ran a profitable business delivering goods to the ports of both nations.

But American neutrality wasn't working. The British insisted American ships stop at British ports on their way to France for inspection and payment of fees. The French General Napoleon threatened to seize ships that followed those orders. All of this came to an abrupt halt in December 1807 when the United States, in an effort to avoid the rising tension between Britain and France, passed the Embargo Act forbidding American ships from sailing into any foreign ports. Since the New England maritime industry depended on international shipping for its livelihood, the results were catastrophic. Tensions also continued to rise between the United States and Britain because of Britain's outrageous practice of Impressment, the seizing of American sailors and forcing them to serve on British ships. Moreover the British encouraged Native American uprisings on the new western frontier. All of these conflicts finally erupted in the unpopular War of 1812.

Anna and the other residents of Groton had not forgotten the massacre at Fort Griswold, and the husbands, brothers, and sons who had fought and died there. Now—more than thirty years later—there was another threat from the British. Commodore Stephen Decatur's frigates and sloop of war were trapped up the Thames River by British warships. The townspeople fled inland, fearful of another British attack.

The story of Anna Warner Bailey's donation of her petticoat on that warm summer day in 1813 has become a treasured Connecticut legend. The startled young soldier carried the petticoat back to the beleaguered Fort Griswold where the jubilant soldiers didn't use it for wadding after all. They ran it up on a pikestaff and planted it on the ramparts of Fort Griswold. Anna Warner Bailey's petticoat was worth more than wadding for guns and cannons. It offered tangible evidence of the gratitude of not just one woman, but of all the citizenry for the soldiers' valiant defense of their homeland.

The British never did attack Fort Griswold or Groton again. After months of remaining barricaded up the Thames River, it was decided that Commodore Decatur's ships should be taken further up the river beyond reach of the enemy and dismantled. His men engaged in an unsucessful land skirmish with British troops, but otherwise saw little action. The blockading British ships were eventually driven out to sea by a fierce snow storm, and the unpopular War of 1812 was finally declared over with the signing of the Treaty of Ghent on December 24, 1814 (ratified on February 17, 1815).

Anna Warner Bailey survived her second war with the British and went on to live a long life with her husband Elijah. She was described by those who knew her as a "kind neighbor, a good friend, and always ready to assist the needy or . . . to relieve the wants of the poor and distressed." But she never got over her antipathy toward the British and spoke about it often throughout her life.

Anna Warner Bailey died in a house fire on January 10, 1851, when she was ninety-two years old. The fame engendered by her heroic and patriotic acts, first during the Revolution and then again during the War of 1812, grew to be legend. It was reported in the local papers that Presidents Monroe and Jackson visited her to thank her for her patriotism, and a branch of the Daughters of the American Revolution bears her name in Connecticut to this day.

Throughout both wars there were many other brave women who faced danger to thwart the enemy and protect their homeland. Anna Warner Bailey epitomized their efforts and bore witness to the fact that valor, bravery, and fierce patriotism were not exclusive to the men of the new nation but were traits shared by all its citizens.

In later years she described the famous petticoat as "a right good article . . . bound with good quality binding"—a perfect description of the owner herself.

Julia Evelina Smith
1792–1886

Abby Hadassah Smith
1797–1878

The Smith Sisters
of Glastonbury

The seven cows mooed plaintively, unaccustomed as they were to being confined in such a small, unfamiliar place. Instead of their spacious home barn, they were enclosed in a rough shed, barely 12 feet by 15 feet. And instead of their loving owners, Julia and Abby Smith, they were being tended to by a stranger who would have little luck winning their affection. Jessie, Daisy, Proxy, Minnie, Bessie, Whitey, and Lily were not simply prized Alderney milk cows, they were considered valuable members of the Smith family. Indeed they were often not happy being milked unless Julia Smith stood where they could see her, offering moral support during the whole proceedings.

Their confinement in the shed had been the cause for much publicity in the small town of Glastonbury, Connecticut, and as they had been led away from their family they had bellowed mournfully. It would be seven long days before they were reunited with the eighth cow in the herd, and once again comfortably lodged in their home barn. And during those seven days they would be transformed from simple (albeit affectionately revered) farm livestock into pawns in a battle over nothing less than the basic tenets of the Constitution of the United States.

Julia and Abby Smith, eighty-one and seventy-six years old respectively, were themselves respected members of the community of Glastonbury, where they had lived their entire lives. The battle over the cows on that cold New Year's Day of 1874 was a culmination of their unwavering devotion to personal rights first framed by the Declaration of Independence and later secured by the Constitution, and its ramifications would echo for many years. The Smith cows were seized in payment for back taxes owed by the two women, taxes which they had refused to pay because they claimed that, since as women they were not allowed to vote and to influence the laws and policies of their country, they were being taxed without representation. The tyranny of taxation without representation had been one of the rallying cries of the battling colonists that had precipitated the Revolutionary War. As far as the Smith sisters were concerned, it was just as valid a claim in 1874 as it had been a hundred years earlier.

Julia Evelina and Abby Hadassah were born into the lively Smith family of Glastonbury at the end of the eighteenth century, fourth and fifth in a line of five sisters. Their mother, Hannah Hickock, had been an only child. Her educated, religious parents had imbued her with an independent spirit and a reverence for intellectual pursuits—qualities that she would in turn inspire in her own daughters. Their father, Zephaniah Hollister, was a Yale graduate who after graduation joined the religious sect of Sandemanianists, or Glasites, a group that required its followers to adhere to strict and bizarre tenets. Sandemanianists did not believe in storing up material wealth on this earth and were admonished not to challenge government officials, since they believed those officials' powers were ordained by God. Zephaniah

Julia Evelina Smith (left) and Abby Hadassah Smith

eventually left the religious life because he believed it was morally wrong to accept money for preaching the gospel. After a brief career in business, he turned to the study of law.

Their father's ultimate choice of profession would later profoundly influence the girls' lives, but it was their mother's deep love of language and scholarship that probably exerted the earliest influence. As a young girl Hannah studied Latin and French and translated books from those languages as a pastime. As a grown woman she learned Italian, wrote poetry, and studied mathematics and astronomy, activities she enjoyed throughout her lifetime.

Perhaps to offset the simplicity of their last name, she and Zephaniah gave their five girls unusual first names: Hancy Zephina, Cyrinthia Sacretia, Laurilla Aleroyla, Julia Evelina (changed from Julietta Abelinda), and Abby Hadassah, names that set them apart from girls with the more popular names of the day and imbued the family with an air of genteel eccentricity. Hannah and Zephaniah disagreed heartily with the common belief of that time that encouraged only a limited education for women. All a young woman needed in the way of education, it was thought, was to learn a little "ciphering" and reading, a little music and art. Such simple studies would make her pleasing to a prospective mate; anything more challenging would make her coarse and unwomanly. Studying advanced subjects would also bring into sharp relief the difference between the life of submission that was ordained for a woman by God and the role of domination over her that was to be enjoyed by her brothers and ultimately by her husband.

Both parents considered these theories to be nonsense. They saw to it that all the girls were thoroughly educated in literature, mathematics, history, languages, and science. They taught them at home, hired tutors, and at times sent them to boarding schools. While much of their time was spent helping with the farm chores, sewing, reading, and performing charitable works, the girls also became familiar with the law through their father's practice. They helped him keep track of his cases, read his law books, and witnessed ceremonies performed in his office adjacent to their home.

Unlike most families, the sisters' lives changed very little as they reached adulthood. None of them married, except for Julia who married late in life after all of her sisters had died. Most never left home, and those who did never stayed away for long. Julia Evelina and Laurilla Aleroyla left for brief tenures as teachers at the Emma Willard School in Troy, New York, but Julia was overcome with homesickness and returned home within a year. Laurilla Aleroyla spent some time teaching French and art in Hartford, but she too eventually returned to live with her sisters.

Each of the girls contributed a special talent to the family unit. Hancy Zephina was a gifted musician and entertained her sisters on the piano. Cyrinthia Sacretia was skilled in needlework and horticulture and maintained the family's gardens. Laurilla Aleroyla was a talented artist whose works graced the walls of their home, and who sketched many of the homes in Glastonbury. Julia Evelina was a gifted writer and spent long hours translating the Bible from Hebrew, Greek, and Latin, eventually translating it five times in a Herculean effort to divine its real meaning. Abby Hadassah was the most domestic of the sisters, and it was she who took on responsibility for the home, but she also wrote poetry—as her mother did—and tended to her garden. All the girls took turns with the housework and shared a deep devotion to charitable works. They were a self-sufficient, cheerful, and accomplished unit, dependent on each other for financial, moral, and social support.

Despite Zephaniah's defection from the ministry, religion played an important role in the sisters' lives. Their father encouraged them to turn to the Bible for guidance, and they took its lessons of brotherly love to heart, especially regarding abolition and the evils of slavery. All the Smiths abhorred slavery. "Anti-slavery is expressed in one short sentence," Abby wrote to a friend, "all men equal before the law. The oppression of the negroes will not cease 'till then." They had long exhibited a charitable concern for the blacks of Glastonbury who, though free, were all very poor. They taught a Sunday school for black men and women, hired black help in their home, and cared for those blacks in town who were ill and destitute. Eventually these activities led in the 1830s to actively working for abolition, circulating petitions against slavery, and joining anti-slavery societies.

When Zephaniah died in 1836 the family of women was left bereft, not just of his company and of his love but of his political influence. Never before had they felt more keenly the difference in the political status of the sexes. Although they were self-sufficient and worked and paid taxes, they could hold no office, testify in no court of law, and vote in no election. As women they were politically powerless and at the mercy of laws that were passed without their consent and over any objections they might have. Zephaniah's death left their political voices muted and their freedom of speech compromised, for petitions and letters signed by women were frequently ignored by legislators, and women were repeatedly refused the right to even speak of these matters in public.

Yet they persisted. They circulated issues of the anti-slavery newspaper *The Charter Oak* and went door to door throughout Glastonbury seeking signatures on anti-slavery petitions. They entertained abolitionists in their home, including the famed William Lloyd Garrison, and members of the family of Prudence Crandall, a young Connecticut woman who had been jailed for opening a school for black girls in nearby Canterbury. Unlike many abolitionists who worked to free the slaves but personally avoided contact with blacks, the Smiths attended their meetings and conventions and openly welcomed blacks into their home.

Sadly, by the time the Emancipation Proclamation was signed on January 1, 1863, two of the Smith women had died and one would soon follow. Hannah had died in 1850, Laurilla in 1857, and Cyrinthia in 1864. While the remaining sisters were heartened by the slaves' freedom, their own disenfranchisement remained a sore point. The sisters found particularly ironic the debate on whether or not to grant freed black men the vote. They who had worked so hard for abolition, and who could claim at least part of the credit for its success, were still without franchise while those whose freedom they had helped to secure might now claim that right. Thus the sisters decided that it was now time to turn their energies to fighting for their own rights, to securing for themselves and all women the "blessings of liberty" promised by the Constitution of the United States.

News of the movement for women's rights would not have escaped the sisters' notice, even in the small town of Glastonbury. Since they were voracious readers of newspapers and periodicals, they must have been aware of the Woman's Rights Convention that had been convened in Seneca Falls, New York, in 1848, and the subsequent conventions that were continuously being held throughout the region. Perhaps they even heard news of Elizabeth Cady Stanton's letter that had been read aloud by Susan B. Anthony at the third National Woman's Rights Convention held in Syracuse, New York, in September 1852. "Should not all women," Susan questioned, "living in States where woman has the right to hold property refuse to pay taxes, so long as she is unrepresented in the government of that State?" But in 1852 the sisters were still busy taking care of the farm and each other and working for abolition. It was not until that goal was reached and the blacks were freed that they turned their energies to the battle for suffrage.

The first skirmish happened in 1869 with a seemingly insignificant highway tax of eighteen dollars that the sisters were asked to pay twice. When their protests to the tax collector fell on deaf ears, Julia, Abby, and Hancy Zephina were incensed, knowing that the men of the town suffered no such injustice. Julia and Abby decided to travel to Hartford to attend the first convention of the Connecticut Woman Suffrage Association. There they hoped they might join forces with other women who were fighting for equal rights and perhaps have their voices heard. At the convention they listened to such electrifying speakers as Elizabeth Cady Stanton, Susan B. Anthony, and Julia Ward Howe, and a sense of righteousness once again found fertile root in their elderly souls. "We came home believing that the women had truth on their side," they later recalled, "but never did it once enter our heads to refuse to pay taxes."

Hancy Zephina's death in 1871 brought a pause to their political activities as the two remaining sisters tried to come to terms with yet another loss. But in 1872 they were forced into action when they discovered that their tax assessment had been arbitrarily increased by one hundred dollars, an increase that was even more galling when they discovered that only two other women of the town had been so charged, and not a single man. Julia recalled the meeting with the tax collector in her book, *Abby Smith and Her Cows With a Report of the Law Case Decided Contrary to Law:*

> I asked him why our assessment was more than last year for we laid up no money and did not intend to. He replied that the assessor had a right to add to our tax as much as he pleased and he had assessed our house and homestead a hundred dollars more. To be sure it increased our tax but little, but what is unjust in least is unjust in much. I inquired if it was done so to any man's property. He looked over his book to see and not a man had his tax raised; there were only two widows in our neighborhood that were so used.

The sisters decided they were tired of paying taxes without having any say in how their money was to be spent. They might be elderly but they were in no way unable to speak their minds. In 1873 Julia and Abby attended the first convention of the American Woman Suffrage Association in New York. Julia was eighty-one years old. Abby was seventy-six. There they again listened to speakers exhort them on the need for women to speak against unjust laws, to rail against taxation without representation, and to petition for the right to vote.

When they returned home Abby decided she would pay a visit to the next town meeting where she would speak her mind and where, she was sure, reason would prevail. "It seemed so unreasonable to us," Abby later wrote to a friend, "that our town should take our property from us whenever they pleased, without asking us about it, that they could not help to see the injustice, if we told them of it in the best way we could."

On November 5, 1873, the two sisters appeared before the Town Meeting of Glastonbury where they were received cordially, and where Abby explained that the sisters only wanted what "every human being wants—control over that which belongs to him." The sisters realized, she explained, that the property of the town was taxed to pay the expenses of the town, but as taxpayers they wished to have a voice in the town's practices.

> We cannot see why we are not just as capable of assisting in managing the affairs of the town as the men are. We cannot possibly see why we have not just as much intelligence . . . or as much capacity for doing business as they have. . . . Is it any more right and just to take a woman's property without her consent than it is to take a man's property without his consent? Is it right because men are the strongest they can go into the women's houses and take their money

from them knowing they cannot resist? . . . Here
where liberty is so highly extolled by every man, one-
half the inhabitants . . . are ruled over by the other
half . . . who can take all they possess. . . . How is
Liberty pleased with such worship? Would she not be
apt to think of her own sex?

But such eloquent protestations were in vain. The men virtually ignored the sisters' pleas, and not long after the tax collector
again returned to their home. This time the sisters refused to pay
any tax, informing him that if the town was planning to take their
property they should start "at the east end," for they wished to preserve the land on which their house stood for as long as they lived.

The dreaded tax collector again visited them on New Year's
Day, 1874, to claim seven of the sisters' eight prized Alderney
cows for back taxes owed in the amount of $101.39. In Julia's
book she reported: "We pleaded hard for a respite, till we could
speak again before the town. We wanted to petition the men, we
said, to let us own our land as they owned theirs, and then we
would willingly pay our taxes; and how much better it would be to
have the money paid freely than to have all this trouble about it."

But the tax man would not be appeased. Julia even entreated
him to "leave two of the cows together so one might not be left
alone." But he refused. "He took seven because he said cows were low
and he wanted enough." After seven miserable days shut up in a
strange shed, the cows were led in a somber parade down the lane to
a signpost where an auction was to be held. Although the men of
Glastonbury would not speak to the sisters, nor acknowledge their
complaints about suffrage, they kept their bids for the cows suspi-
ciously low, allowing the sisters' tenant, Mr. Kellog, to buy four of
the cows, and returned the other three to the sisters without payment. The Smith sisters were respected in the town. They caused the
men embarrassment, but they did not elicit outright enmity. Not yet.

In a politically astute move, Abby had sent a copy of her November speech at Town Hall to the *Hartford Courant*, which had printed it in its entirety. The *Springfield Republican* in nearby Massachusetts reported the case as well. When accounts of the seizure of the cows appeared in both newspapers, the Smith sisters' defiance of what they considered to be unfair taxation was compared to the bravery of those who had conducted the Boston Tea Party a century before. The *Springfield Republican* reporter admonished his readers that "it will not be creditable if Abby Smith and her sister are left to stand alone . . . to fight the battle of principle unaided."

The following March the tax collector again returned to the Smith homestead, and when the sisters again refused to pay any tax he announced he would begin seizing their land, although he knew full well that such an action was illegal. The law clearly stated that personal property—furniture, paintings, household items—must be seized before any land. But in direct defiance of that law, the tax collector announced that he was putting their land up for auction on June 20.

On April 6, 1874, Abby and Julia again attended the Town Meeting, but this time they were refused permission to speak. Undaunted, the sisters left the building and climbed atop a wagon that was parked outside to give their speech. Abby spoke first. She reminded her listeners that she and her sister had heretofore been loyal citizens who paid more tax than most men of the town. She reiterated their stand that they would pay no tax until they could vote. Julia joined her in speaking a few sentences. But again, all was in vain. On June 20 Julia and Abby watched as the tax collector illegally auctioned off eleven acres of their best meadowland to their neighbor, whom they knew had always coveted it. For the back tax of $78.35 the neighbor obtained land worth over $2,000.

Thus followed several years that found the elderly sisters filing suits and answering appeals, suffering through three trials and several careless lawyers in attempts to get their land back. When their lawyer deserted them they returned to reading Zephaniah's law books, studying law themselves in despair of ever finding a competent attorney to defend them. The poignant story of two elderly ladies being persecuted by their town while standing firm on principle sold papers everywhere it was printed, and money and support came from all over the nation. The sisters themselves were surprised by the outcry and took heart from the groundswell of public opinion in their favor. An average of twenty-four letters a week arrived at their home, many including donations of cash and checks, and more than thirty newspapers "noticed them favorably." Abby wrote to a friend: "Our letters from all parts of the Union would astonish anyone, we think, as well as ourselves. With a voice of strength, for it is a voice of unity, they tell us to go on, for we are standing on the right ground, and they will aid us in every way."

In May 1874 Abby spoke before the Woman Suffrage Committee of the state legislature of Connecticut. Suffrage leaders took notice of the sisters, wrote to them, and visited them, and they were invited to speak at other suffrage conventions and meetings. Isabella Beecher Hooker, sister to Harriet Beecher Stowe and a noted suffragist, donated five dollars to the sisters' defense fund. Lucy Stone traveled to Glastonbury to meet them and afterward wrote: "Here some day, as to Bunker Hill, will come men and women who are reverent of the great principle of the consent of the governed, and will hold at its true value the part that these sisters have taken in solving the meaning of a representative government."

The elderly sisters complemented each other beautifully. Tall, spare Abby made most of the speeches while the smaller, more reticent Julia concentrated on the writing. In 1855 Julia had completed her final translation of the Bible, a labor that had taken her eight long years. At the time she had no intention of having her translation published, but in 1876, reasoning that its publication might give evidence of what a "mere woman might accomplish," she arranged for its publication with a firm from Hartford. In 1877 she also released her book *Abby Smith and Her Cows With a Report of the Law Case Decided Contrary to Law*, which reported the sisters' tribulations in clear and minute detail.

In 1876 the sisters finally won their last court case when a judge decided that the town had indeed erred in seizing their land before their personal possessions. Although they still had to pay taxes and still could not vote, the sisters continued to press the legislature for change and continued to write, speak, and lobby for the rights that were denied them.

When Abby died in 1878, Julia was devastated and in her loneliness hastily married Judge Amos Parker, an attorney who lived in New Hampshire. Amos had written to Julia after reading her translation of the Bible, and the two had struck up a friendship that later blossomed into romance. But the marriage was not a happy one, and when Julia died in 1886 and was buried with her parents and sisters, her gravestone bore only her maiden name.

Abby and Julia Smith and their family had spent their entire lives working for justice, first for the enslaved blacks and later for women. At an age that would find most resting from the labors of a long, busy life they worked harder than ever—writing, traveling, speaking, and lobbying for freedom from oppression. They irritated legislators, inspired suffragists, and offered newspaper editors a seemingly unending source of entertaining copy.

Their humor and wit often rescued them from despair. When they reported they had named two cows Taxey and Votey and a calf Abigail Adams, it only added to their popular appeal. But beneath the humor, and their love of the spotlight, smoldered a deep and unswerving devotion to personal freedom and to securing equal rights for all under the law, and they followed those goals until the end of their lives. Abby's first speech at the Town Meeting in November 1873 sums up their beliefs eloquently: "Do we not stand on an equality with them and with every man in this assembly before the law of God? God is a God of justice; men and women stand alike in his sight; he has but one law for both . . . to which both shall be accountable alike. Let each rise if they can by their own ability and put no obstructions in their way."

PRUDENCE CRANDALL

1803–1890

Abolitionist Schoolmistress

$\mathcal{T}$he young schoolmistress stood straight and tall to face the court. As the judge read the charges against her she did not flinch. As she had expected, her case was bound over to a court in a neighboring town, and she was advised she must post a $150 bond or suffer imprisonment in the county jail until her trial, a good six weeks away. "I cannot pay," she told the judge. "You will have to put me in jail."

But this was Canterbury, Connecticut, in June 1833, a God-fearing, prosperous little New England town. No one in his right mind would think of arresting the local schoolmistress and forcing her to spend time in jail. There were unconfirmed but disturbing rumors that she would be confined in the former cell of a man who had recently been executed for strangling his wife. Even as he spoke the harsh words that would imprison her, the judge was certain one of her friends would come forward to post bail to relieve her of this grave indignity, and at the same time relieve him of the embarrassment she was causing him.

Prudence Crandall

But the judge was wrong. Prudence Crandall stood alone. To the astonishment of all concerned, not a single person came forward to post her bail. Reluctantly, the judge ordered the sheriff to take her away to the county jail in nearby Brooklyn, Connecticut, where she was politely shown to a large, newly whitewashed cell. She was allowed one companion, her friend Anna Benson, to keep her company. The cell door clanged shut behind the two trembling young women, as they unknowingly entered a disturbing and inglorious passage in the annals of Connecticut history.

Although it was Prudence Crandall's first and only time in jail, it would certainly not be her last brush with the law. By defiantly maintaining a school to educate young black women, she would break the laws of the State of Connecticut again and again, risking imprisonment, the ruination of her business, and the animosity of her community. But her Quaker soul told her that slavery, with its related discriminations, was sinful, so she would continue to wage a valiant fight against it. Let the people see that she would gladly suffer for her beliefs. If the State of Connecticut was jailing young women for the crime of educating blacks, let Prudence Crandall be the first one in the cell door!

Prudence was born on September 3, 1803, in Hopkinton, Rhode Island, the second of four children of Quaker parents, Pardon and Esther Crandall. Her paternal grandfather, John Crandall, had arrived in the Massachusetts Colony in 1635 but had moved to Rhode Island after quarreling with the settlement's founders over his Anabaptist faith. His son Pardon married Esther Carpenter whose father, Hezekiah, owned a prosperous iron foundry. Hezekiah built a house for the newlyweds, expecting them to stay near him indefinitely, and all four children were born in the comfortable farmhouse in Hopkinton. But Pardon eventually came to resent his father-in-law's influence over his family, especially over Esther. When Prudence was ten years old he abruptly moved the family 30 miles away to the small village of Canterbury, Connecticut.

The family prospered in Canterbury. The two Crandall boys grew up to go into business and study medicine. Prudence was sent to a Quaker boarding school in Providence whose founder, Moses Brown, was an ardent abolitionist. There she received a comprehensive education, quite unusual for most girls of that time, which included instruction in mathematics, Latin, and the sciences. The school welcomed both boys and girls of varied religions and family backgrounds, encouraged them to become "broad minded citizens," and offered scholarships to poor children. Even as a young girl, Prudence had exhibited an affinity for new and progressive ideas, and the school and its founder no doubt contributed to the further development of this trait.

When she left Brown Seminary in 1830, Prudence taught briefly in a boarding school in Plainfield, Connecticut, and in 1831 was asked by the citizens of Canterbury to open a school for the young ladies of their town. The idea for such a school made eminent sense for the citizens of Canterbury, as it would save them the expense of sending their daughters to more distant boarding schools and at the same time would lend the town an air of progressive respectability. The residents were confident in Prudence's ability to run such a school, so confident that one offered a mortgage of $1,500 to help her purchase an imposing white mansion conveniently situated on the village green. A board of visitors was created to support and counsel her. One of the leading members of the board was attorney Andrew T. Judson, whose house was directly across the village green. Prudence's younger sister, Almira, would act as her assistant.

The Canterbury Female Boarding School opened in the fall of 1831, with about twenty students in attendance. The curriculum was ambitious, ranging from English grammar and geography to moral philosophy and astronomy. Tuition was twenty-five dollars per quarter. For the first year Prudence enjoyed the comfort of full acceptance and support from the town of Canterbury, and her bonneted, well-dressed students were a welcomed sight as they strolled two by two through the village on their afternoon walks.

Prudence employed as household help a young black woman, Mariah Davis. Mariah was engaged to Charles Harris, who was an ardent follower of the abolitionist William Lloyd Garrison, and whose father was a sales agent for Garrison's newspaper, *The Liberator.* Mariah freely shared copies of *The Liberator* with Prudence, who read them late at night while her students slept. Within the pages of *The Liberator,* William Lloyd Garrison's fiery anti-slavery rhetoric reaffirmed her Quaker beliefs that slavery and its attendant oppression of blacks was a sin. "Hereafter it will be remembered against us that we oppressed and treated cruelly so many of our brethren, only because of the tincture of their skin," Garrison wrote.

Prudence's abolitionist beliefs, which had most likely taken root during her school days under the tutelage of Moses Brown, were now further encouraged by her readings in *The Liberator.* So when Mariah's sister Sarah approached Prudence and asked to be allowed to attend her school, it seemed for Prudence a perfect opportunity to put those beliefs into action. Sarah's goal was to become educated enough to open a school for other young black women. After a brief hesitancy, Prudence welcomed her as a student in the school in the fall of 1832.

It was a wonderful opportunity for Sarah, as advanced learning for young black women her age was then nonexistent in Connecticut. Despite the fact that there were large black communities in Hartford and nearby Providence, Rhode Island, there were no black colleges or secondary schools. Attempts to open a school for blacks in New Haven the previous year had met with dismal failure. Black children's education usually ended in the local elementary school; education beyond the primary grades was thought by many to be a waste of time and resources, since it was assumed by many whites that blacks could never be their intellectual equals.

But Prudence thought otherwise. If she could educate Sarah, then Sarah could in turn educate other young black women, thus helping them move ahead to take their rightful place in society. Who could possibly object to that? Prudence was soon to discover that practically everyone in the town objected, and they showed their displeasure in myriad unpleasant ways.

It began with polite visits from her students' parents, voicing their disapproval and urging her to reconsider her decision. The board of visitors, led by her neighbor, Andrew T. Judson, expressed its immense displeasure. If she did not remove the black girl from the school, they would be forced to withdraw their own daughters and the school, which had heretofore enjoyed such success, would fail.

Prudence was not to be swayed. "Let it sink then," she replied to her visitors, "for I will not turn her out." Indeed, their threats only seemed to inspire in her an even greater spirit of daring. In January 1833 she quietly met with William Lloyd Garrison in Boston, asking if he might introduce her to black families who would be interested in sending their daughters to her school. She traveled to Providence and then on to New York, meeting with black families and with abolitionists such as the wealthy Arthur Tappan, who had provided funds for the ill-fated New Haven school, and activists Henry and George Benson. Everywhere she went she met with support laced with concern. No schools for blacks had met with success before, despite the need.

Prudence returned home to Canterbury both encouraged and resolute, and on a cold February day in 1833 she summoned her student body and stunned them with the announcement that all her white students were to be immediately dismissed. Beginning in early April, her school would admit young black women only. On

March 2, 1833, the following advertisement appeared in *The Liberator:*

PRUDENCE CRANDALL

*Principal of the Canterbury, (Conn.) Female
Boarding School*

RETURNS her most sincere thanks to those who have patronized her School, and would give information that on the first Monday of April next her School will be opened for the reception of young Ladies and little Misses of color. The branches taught are as follows: Reading, Writing, Arithmetic, English Grammar, Geography, History, Natural and Moral Philosophy, Chemistry, Astronomy, Drawing and Painting, Music on the Piano, together with the French language.

Both Prudence's family and the entire town were shocked. A town meeting was hastily called on March 9, 1833, and both Justice of the Peace Rufus Adams and Andrew T. Judson spoke vehemently against the school. They warned the law-abiding citizens of Canterbury that all manner of social horror might be unleashed upon them by such a school, " . . . the obvious tendency of which would be to collect within the town of Canterbury large numbers of persons from other States whose characters and habits might be various and unknown to us, thereby rendering insecure the persons, property and reputation of our citizens."

With heated rhetoric they cautioned their fellow citizens that an influx of young black women from other states would strain the local economy and lower property values. Once educated, they might encourage other members of their families to move to Canterbury.

Even more appalling, they might aspire to marry white men, thus fulfilling one of the most dreaded fears of the day—amalgamation of blacks into the white race.

Reverend Samuel J. May was a minister from the nearby community of Brooklyn, Connecticut, and was sensitive to the abolitionist cause. When he first heard of Prudence's plans for the school, he wrote to her offering his assistance, asking that she "command my services in any way in which you think I can be useful to you." Prudence decided not to attend the town meeting, and instead asked May to represent her. She also asked abolitionist Arnold Buffum of the New England Anti-Slavery Society to join Samuel May at the meeting. Both men carried letters of introduction to the moderator of the meeting, stating that they were authorized to speak for Prudence, and further stating that she would abide by any compromise they might negotiate with the citizens of the town, including moving the school to another location.

But the letters were little more than a waste of time. Neither May nor Buffum was allowed to speak. After the meeting they made an admirable attempt to explain Prudence's position, but few would listen. The townspeople were frightened by Andrew T. Judson's dire warnings. They had closed their heads and hearts against Prudence and her school and would hear nothing in her favor.

In early April the black girls began to arrive from Providence, New York, Boston, and Philadelphia, fifteen or twenty in all. They were well-dressed, some from well-to-do families, eager to begin their studies. But the warmth of the welcome shown to them by Samuel May, Prudence, Almira, and Sarah was countered by a cold wall of hatred from the rest of the town that no joy in education and learning could ever melt.

Life then became very difficult for Prudence, her family, and her students. Manure was dumped in her well and smeared on her house and steps. The grocer refused to sell her food, the town doctor refused to treat the girls' illnesses, and the Congregational Church, despite its obvious commitment to brotherly love, refused to allow them in the door. Pardon Crandall brought them barrels of water from his own well and transported the girls in his wagon to distant churches to worship on Sundays. But even Pardon was not immune from censure by the town and was warned that he would be fined for simply visiting his daughter. Fines would begin at one hundred dollars and be doubled for each subsequent visit.

Prudence remained outwardly calm throughout, continuing to teach and care for her students, firm in her belief that she was following the right and noble course. But such calm further infuriated her opponents. An obsolete vagrancy law was evoked, which provided that the selectmen of a town could order deported anyone not an inhabitant of the state. If said person refused to leave, they could be fined $1.67 a day, for every week they remained. If the accused had not paid the fine and had not left town after ten days, they could be "whipped on the naked body not exceeding ten stripes." Knowing such a fine would be impossibly expensive for Prudence to pay for each of her students, her abolitionist friends posted a bond in the amount of $10,000 to avoid the impossible horror of having one of the girls publicly whipped.

On May 24, 1833, the State of Connecticut passed the Black Law, which provided: "No person shall set up or establish in this State any school, academy or literary institution for the instruction or education of colored persons who are not inhabitants of this state . . . nor harbor or board any colored person who is not an inhabitant of any town in this State without the consent in writing, first obtained of the majority of the civil authority and also of the Selectmen of the town in which such school, academy or literary institution is situated." Now, to its immense delight, the community of Canterbury had the state legislature behind them, and news of the passage of the Black Law was met with great joy in the town. Bells were rung. Cannons were fired. Penalties for violation of the law were severe. Prudence was warned that if she did not comply she would be jailed.

Thus, on June 27, after a brief hearing, Prudence Crandall found herself in her barren jail cell, a young Quaker woman carrying the banner of the rights of blacks to an education in Connecticut on her slender shoulders. She knew full well that her friends would not bail her out—indeed they had planned together not to do so. Samuel J. May, in his *Some Recollections of Our Antislavery Conflict,* told how he himself prepared the cell for her with a fresh, clean mattress from his own home. He met her at the jail and quietly offered her a last reprieve, which she refused, as he knew she would. "If you now hesitate, if you dread the gloomy place so much as to wish to be saved from it, I will give bonds for you even now." "Oh no," she replied, "I am only afraid they will *not* put me into jail."

Prudence and Anna Benson were released the next day, accepting bond posted by Anna's father, George. The trial was set for August 23, 1833. Prudence and Samuel May were discouraged, but their spirits rose after receiving a letter from Arthur Tappan, the wealthy and influential abolitionist, in which he expressed his appreciation for the work both Samuel and Prudence were doing to further abolition and the rights of blacks and offered his substantial financial support. "Consider me your banker," he wrote May, "spare no necessary expense. Command the services of the ablest lawyers." In addition to paying the bill for Prudence's attorneys, he also provided funds for May to begin publication of *The Unionist,* a newspaper that reported the events in Canterbury and lent support to Prudence and the cause of abolition.

In *The Unionist* Samuel May at last had an instrument to report first-hand on the attacks by the community upon the school—the rocks thrown, the insults and abuse hurled at the young women, the failed attempts to burn down the school. So confident were the publishers that their stand against slavery and abuse of blacks was correct that they even printed letters from the opposition, including their main detractor, Andrew T. Judson!

Prudence Crandall would suffer through three trials in all. The first, held in August of that year in nearby Brooklyn, Connecticut, sought to prove that she had broken the newly passed Black Law and had "with force and arms" harbored young black women from other states in her school for the purpose of educating them without first obtaining proper permission from the "civil authority" of the town. The prosecution further maintained that "colored persons . . . were not by the Constitution recognized as citizens."

The defense admitted that Prudence had violated this law but countered that free blacks were indeed citizens and were allowed all the rights of "free movement and education" that they might have enjoyed in the states they came from. Thus, they stated, the Black Law was unconstitutional. After several hours of deliberation the trial resulted in a hung jury.

The second trial was held in October of that year and was presided over by Chief Justice of the State Supreme Court David Daggett, who was well known for his opposition to the emancipation of blacks and strong support of the Black Law. From the beginning he counseled the jury that, in his mind "slaves, free blacks and Indians" were not citizens. "The African race," he said, "are essentially a degraded caste of inferior rank and condition in society. . . . I am bound by my duty to say they are not citizens." This time the jury took his instructions to heart and found Prudence guilty. That decision was later appealed to the Supreme Court of Errors in Hartford and was ultimately overturned when the court ruled that the prosecution had not provided sufficient evidence.

The constitutional question raised during Prudence Crandall's trials of whether or not free blacks were citizens would continue to trouble the country for many years to come. In 1857, deciding the case of *Dred Scott v. Sanford*, the Supreme Court of the United States would use Judge Daggett's opinion as a basis for its decision that "slaves are not citizens of any state or of the United States." The entire question would not be settled until after the country was virtually torn apart by the Civil War and the Fourteenth Amendment to the Constitution was ratified in 1868, stating that "all persons born or naturalized in the United States . . . are citizens of the United States and of the State wherein they reside."

In September 1834 Prudence Crandall married a young abolitionist minister, Calvin Philleo, and became a second mother to his three children. The newlyweds postponed a wedding trip, as school was still in session. But the Canterbury Female Boarding School was not to be in session for long. The town continued its harassment—the windows were shattered by rocks and the house set afire. Finally, on September 9, 1834, a group of armed thugs surrounded the school, shattered over ninety window panes, and beat the walls in. Prudence finally gave up. The school was closed. Their good friend Samuel May was summoned and asked to give notice to the girls. His account of the evening was poignant and moving:

> Never before had I felt so deeply sensible of the cruelty of the persecution which had been carried on for eighteen months in that New England village against a family of defenseless females. Twenty harmless, well-behaved girls whose only offense against the peace of the community was that they had come together there to obtain useful knowledge and moral

culture were to be told that they had better go away because, forsooth, the house in which they dwelt would not be protected by the guardians of the town, the conservators of the peace, the officers of justice, the men of influence in the village. . . . The words almost blistered on my lips. I felt ashamed of Canterbury, ashamed of Connecticut, ashamed of my country, ashamed of my color.

Prudence and her family moved to New York and, later, to Illinois. The marriage was not a happy one, and when Philleo died in 1874 Prudence moved with her brother Hezekiah to Elk Falls, Kansas. There she led a simple life, teaching young girls, supporting women's suffrage, and dabbling in spiritualism, still asserting her own unique spirit of opposition to conventional thinking. She died in 1890. She was eighty-seven years old.

Prudence Crandall's time spent in the national spotlight was short—barely more than three years—yet it was remarkably effective. She is remembered as one who dared to fight a firmly entrenched system of oppression of blacks, not with guns or violence, but with the mightier weapons of education and her own personal courage. Freedom, she believed, did not belong only to those with white skin—freedom was the right of everyone, especially freedom to pursue an education, for only through education could anyone be totally free. She was not above risking her own personal liberty to further those beliefs.

Prudence's school may have gone down in defeat but the abolition movement in Connecticut grew in strength and influence in its wake. The infamous Black Law was repealed in 1838, only five years after it was passed, and Connecticut supported and ratified the Fourteenth Amendment to the Constitution in 1868. In 1886, four years before she died, the State of Connecticut attempted to make amends to Prudence by awarding her a pension in the amount of $400 a year, a sum she received until her death. On October 1, 1995, in honor of her efforts to promote the civil rights of all of Connecticut's citizens, she was named Connecticut's State Heroine.

"My whole life has been one of opposition," she once admitted, and in the end that spirit of opposition is what ultimately carried her to greatness.

HARRIET BEECHER STOWE

1811–1896

Author, Reformer, and Abolitionist

*T*he Boston Music Hall was filled with the dulcet sounds of music and poetry that cold January day, the first of 1863, but despite the tranquility of the program a frisson of excitement and anticipation ran through the crowd. Weary with the cares of the Civil War, the people waited expectantly for news that their president had signed the Emancipation Proclamation, a move they hoped might bring the war to an end.

A hush descended on the crowd as a well-dressed gentleman stepped to the center stage. The telegram had finally come telling them what they were waiting to hear—President Abraham Lincoln had signed the Emancipation Proclamation. The slaves at last were free. The walls of the concert hall fairly shook with the joyful shouts and cheers of the audience.

In the last row of the balcony, a small, modestly dressed woman sat quietly, enjoying the revelry. No one knew better than she did what it was costing the nation to fight this war. Three of her nephews and her own son were on the battlefield. She herself

HARRIET BEECHER STOWE CENTER, HARTFORD, CONNECTICUT

Harriet Beecher Stowe

had worked tirelessly to encourage the president to free the slaves and end the war. Now at least part of her dream was coming to fruition.

Suddenly someone noticed her presence. Rumor ran like wildfire throughout the concert hall that Harriet Beecher Stowe, the author of *Uncle Tom's Cabin,* was in the audience. The crowd called her name and she rose to answer its call. Now the cheers were for her and she bore the adulation modestly, in awe herself of what her work had accomplished. For in the eyes of her countrymen and indeed the eyes of the president himself, this woman had used her pen to change their world.

Harriet Beecher was born on June 14, 1811, into a family that would eventually number eleven children. (A sister also named Harriet had died in infancy three years earlier.) Her father was Lyman Beecher, a Presbyterian minister with Calvinistic leanings who had been born and raised in Guilford, Connecticut. Her mother was Roxana Foote, a granddaughter of General Ward who had served under George Washington. Roxana and Lyman would have two more children after Harriet, both sons. After serving as a minister in East Hampton on Long Island, Lyman moved his growing family to Litchfield, Connecticut, to preach in the Litchfield Congregational Church.

Lyman's salary was modest and the family was never far from the edge of poverty. To augment their meager income, Roxana took in boarders from a local school for young ladies. She was a simple, strong woman who enjoyed gardening and reading aloud to her children. But in 1815 Roxana was suddenly taken ill and died. Two years after her death Lyman married Harriet Porter who gave him four more children, a girl and three boys, one of whom would also die in infancy.

Lyman was a revivalist, a moral reformer who was convinced that it was his sacred duty to make as many converts for God and thus to save as many souls as was humanly possible. While the strict adherents to Calvinism believed in the doctrine of predestination—the belief that God grants salvation only to the chosen or elect—Lyman preferred to teach that humans had a responsibility for their own salvation. To this end he preached loud, fiery sermons designed to "scorch" his congregations into repenting their sins and thus saving their own souls. Lyman loved Harriet and all his children, but he particularly treasured his sons. Since girls were not allowed to speak in public, only the boys could become ministers and help him spread God's word; six of them did just that.

Strict and severe by nature, Harriet Porter never established a very warm relationship with her stepchildren. Perhaps she was overcome by caring for such a large family, but her cool nature caused the children to turn toward each other for love and affection. For mothering Harriet turned to her older sister, Catharine, and for friendship to her closest brothers, George, four years older, and Henry Ward, two years younger. Throughout her life she was to be closest to these siblings, especially Henry Ward.

Harriet attended the local Litchfield school, where she learned at an early age to both enjoy and to master the written word. She was a voracious reader and a prolific writer. When she was only twelve she received high praise for her composition "Can the Immortality of the Soul Be Proved by the Light of Nature?"—an argument so well constructed and produced that it would be far beyond the understanding of most twelve-year-olds today. Upon hearing her composition read aloud at a school assembly, Lyman was filled with pride but mournfully noted that if only she had been a boy, he could have given her $100 as a reward.

Like all the Beecher children, Harriet was consumed with anxiety about her own spiritual health, fearing herself to be sinful beyond redemption. When she was thirteen, her sister Catharine reported to their father that Harriet had written to her of a wish to die young "and let the remembrance of me and my faults perish in the grave, rather than live, as I fear I do, a trouble to everyone." She recommended to their father that Harriet join her in Hartford and attend the school Catharine had founded, the Hartford Female Seminary. She hoped that Harriet would find "cheerful and amusing friends" at school who could help her overcome her depression.

Harriet attended the seminary and within the next few years began teaching there. Her sister kept her busy—teaching all day and studying through the evening in an attempt to stay two steps ahead of her students. By the age of seventeen she seemed to have tamed her religious demons and to have found spiritual peace, for the next few years saw her make new friends and find society "full of interest and pleasure." This development of a more outgoing personality allowed her the freedom to observe and develop strong opinions about the behavior of others, a talent that would influence her writing for the rest of her life.

In 1832 Lyman Beecher was offered the presidency of Lane Theological Seminary in Cincinnati, Ohio, and most of his large family decided to accompany him on the move west, including Harriet. In Cincinnati she befriended Eliza Stowe, wife of Calvin Stowe, a professor of Biblical literature. Harriet, Catharine, and the Stowes joined the Semi-Colon Club, a social group that offered members the opportunity to submit their writings for criticism. Encouraged by the group, Harriet submitted a piece to the *Western Monthly Magazine*, and to her surprise, she won a fifty-dollar first prize in the competition for "A New England Sketch," an essay describing her father's Uncle Lot. She began to devote more of her free time to writing.

In 1834 she journeyed east to attend the graduation of her brother Henry Ward from Amherst College. When she returned home to Cincinnati, she discovered that her good friend Eliza Stowe had died of cholera. Harriet and Eliza's husband, Calvin, turned to each other, seeking comfort from their loss of friend and wife. A deep affection developed, and on January 6, 1836, they were married.

Calvin Stowe was nine years older than Harriet. At thirty-three he was balding and overweight and given to wide emotional swings. The marriage was strained by both a scarcity of money and the arrival of four children within four years, twin girls in 1836, and two sons, born in 1838 and 1840. With Calvin often away on business, Harriet found herself lost in a world of domestic chaos. She wrote to a friend that she was "but a mere drudge with few ideas beyond babies and housekeeping." But despite caring for a growing family she found snatches of time to write, and in 1834 Harper & Brothers published *The Mayflower*, a collection of her sketches and stories. The small literary success not only brought her needed funds but encouraged her to consider writing as a serious endeavor. She determined that she would set aside a room of her own where she could write, free from domestic responsibilities.

But these lofty ideals were difficult to attain. Like working women throughout the ages, Harriet faced a conflict between her desire to develop her craft, to care for her growing family, and to protect her own fragile health. A fifth child was born in 1843 and a sixth in 1849, a boy who died of cholera in infancy. In 1850, when Harriet was pregnant with her seventh child, the family moved back to New England, where Calvin was offered a post at Bowdoin College in Brunswick, Maine. To augment his meager salary, Harriet opened a small school in her home and continued to submit articles and sketches for publication. The family finally began to experience some financial and domestic tranquility.

Even more compelling to Harriet than the solution of her own domestic problems was the growing crisis over the subject of slavery. In Cincinnati the family had lived just across the Ohio River from the slave-owning state of Kentucky. Although Harriet had hated slavery from childhood, she and her siblings had adopted their father Lyman's somewhat passive position on the subject. He was not in favor of slavery certainly, but he did not advocate for complete abolition. Better to take things gradually, Lyman recommended, even perhaps see the slaves relocated to Africa to the new nation of Liberia. But what Harriet had seen in Cincinnati changed her mind forever.

She had watched, horrified, as boats filled with chained slaves passed by on the Ohio River, traveling south to sell their cargo to the highest bidder. She had visited friends on a plantation in Kentucky and witnessed first-hand the conditions under which slaves lived. When a young woman in her employ confessed to Harriet that she was a runaway slave, Harriet helped the young woman escape with her son to a safe house on the Underground Railroad. Here at last, she thought as she arranged for the woman's passage, was something concrete she could do to fight that hated system.

Her brother Charles had written to her from the South with accounts of the savage beatings and cruelties he had seen visited upon the slaves. She had heard first-hand from her Aunt Mary about the indignities visited upon slave women by Mary's own husband on his plantation in the West Indies. But nothing galvanized Harriet's feelings against slavery more passionately than the passage in 1850 of the Fugitive Slave Act.

The Fugitive Slave Act was passed by Congress as part of the Compromise of 1850 and required citizens in the North to aid directly in the capture and return of any black person that slaveholders claimed to be a slave. Special commissioners were appointed to accost the suspects and were paid five dollars if the alleged slave was released and ten dollars if they were sent to their claimant in the South. The captured blacks were denied the right to trial, and even free blacks were sometimes arrested and enslaved. The Fugitive

Slave Act infuriated the northern states because it made it mandatory for both free states and the federal government to actively participate in the slave trade.

At the time of the passage of the Fugitive Slave Act, Harriet and her family were just getting settled in their new home in Brunswick, Maine. Her indignation knew no bounds, but she was at a loss to know what to do about it. Her sister-in-law, Mrs. Edward Beecher, felt the same way and wrote to Harriet in frustration and indignation. Mrs. Edward Beecher also wrote to her nephew, Charles Stowe. In his biography of his mother, *The Life of Harriet Beecher Stowe*, Charles recalled the letter he received from his aunt. Mrs. Beecher wrote, "What can I do? I thought. Not much myself, but I know one who can. So I wrote several letters to your mother telling her of various heart-rending events caused by the enforcement of the Fugitive Slave Law. I remember distinctly saying in one of them, 'Now Hattie, if I could use a pen as you can I would write something that would make this whole nation feel what an accursed thing slavery is.'"

Charles Stowe described his mother's reaction to her own letter from Mrs. Beecher: "When Mrs. Stowe read the letter she rose up from her chair, crushing the letter in her hand, and with an expression on her face that stamped itself on the mind of her child said: 'I will write something. I will if I live.' "

Months passed before she finally found time to act. A seventh child, a son, was born, and Harriet's life bustled with family responsibilities. But one Sunday morning in February 1851 she was sitting in church listening to the sermon when a vision suddenly came to her. She saw clearly an elderly slave being beaten to death by his overseers, wracked with pain but still convinced that his Lord had not forgotten him. The vision so stunned her with its clarity and passion that she rushed home and wrote the whole scene down on a piece of brown wrapping paper. When she had finished she gathered her young children around her and read the story to them. The children promptly burst into tears. "Oh, Mamma, slavery is the most cruel thing in the world," her son cried, and Harriet knew at once that she had found the right voice. Uncle Tom was born.

But again her busy life intervened. She put the papers aside while she struggled to keep her family fed, clean, and healthy. It wasn't until a month later that Calvin found the scrawled notes on the brown wrapping paper on her desk. When he read them, he was obviously moved. "What is this?" he asked. "It is the end of the story," Harriet told him, "the story of Uncle Tom." "You must finish it," he told her. "The Lord intends it so."

When the first chapter—the beginning of the story—was written, she sent it to the *National Era* magazine, an anti-slavery publication whose editor agreed to publish it in twelve monthly installments and to pay her $300. The first installment appeared on June 5, 1851. She called the story *Uncle Tom's Cabin, or Life Among the Lowly.*

Harriet was now truly overwhelmed with responsibilities. With deadlines for chapters and so many children to care for, she finally turned to her older sister Catharine for help.

Catharine Beecher was enjoying a flourishing writing career of her own. She was a self-professed expert on all manner of domestic science, including but not limited to teaching, home-making, and child rearing, all despite the fact that she had never married, had never established her own home, and had never had any children. Yet her writings were enormously successful. She encouraged women to take pride in their position as wives and mothers and to work diligently to expand their powers within that domestic sphere. She encouraged education for women but stopped short of advocating women's suffrage, arguing that it would undermine respect for woman's traditional role of wife and mother. Her most famous work was *A Treatise on Domestic Economy*, published in 1841.

Now Catharine stepped in to help her sister, moving into her home, virtually taking command of the whole family, including Calvin. She stunned them by insisting on starting a small school in the family parlor to augment their income. Each day she sent Harriet off with Calvin to write in his office at Bowdoin while she tended to the home and the children. It is entirely doubtful that Harriet could have successfully finished *Uncle Tom's Cabin* without the help and support of her sister.

The story was so popular with readers that the editor of the *National Era* asked Harriet to submit a chapter weekly instead of monthly. Even with Catharine's help Harriet had to scramble to keep up. When one chapter was late and the *National Era* went to press without it, there was a cry of protest from readers. The final chapter was written and delivered in April 1852, and the whole manuscript was published in two volumes by Boston publisher John P. Jewett soon after.

The book form of *Uncle Tom's Cabin* enjoyed even more startling success than the magazine articles. As her son Charles reported in his biography of his mother, "The fears of the author as to whether or not her book would be read were quickly dispelled. Three thousand copies were sold the very first day, a second edition was issued the following week . . . and within a year over three hundred thousand copies of the book had been issued and sold in this country. Almost in a day the poor professor's wife had become the most talked-of woman in the world. . . . Within four months from the time her book was published it had yielded her $10,000 in royalties."

Harriet and her family were freed from poverty at last. *Uncle Tom's Cabin* would go on to become an American classic, translated into sixty languages and sold and read around the world.

In the more than 150 years since its publication, there has been no shortage of analysis of *Uncle Tom's Cabin*, both critical and supportive. Students, educators, writers, and politicians have analyzed its character construction, its writing style, its symbolism, and its sociological impact on American society. For more than a century the literary community has sought to pin down the reason it became a classic of American literature and to analyze exactly why its effect on the nation was so profound.

From the first chapter, where we find two men discussing in chilling and casual detail the sale of another, to the last page, where a repentant slave owner gives each of his slaves their certificates of freedom, Harriet's goal as author is clearly to bring home to her readers in vivid and horrifying detail the human aspect of slavery. Repulsed by the acceptance and legality of slavery, she sought to sting the social conscience of what she considered to be a complacent and morally decaying society with a true picture of its own soul. She showed children torn from their mother's arms, husbands and wives sold apart, women sexually abused—all perfectly legal actions in a country that claimed to be infused with Christian values. In the narrative white women console themselves that black women don't really love their children as much as they themselves do, asserting, "They are a degraded race and always will be." Slave traders protest that since what they do is perfectly legal they are no different from the wealthy slave buyer. As the slave trader Haley remarked, "So long as your grand folks wants to buy men and women I'm as good as they are. Taint any meaner sellin' on 'em than 't is buyin' em."

The underlying theme continually stressed the conflict between religious and civil law, between good and evil. Harriet's characterization of women often pictured them as brave saviors, from the Quaker Mrs. Bird who swore she would not uphold the unjust law of slavery ("It's a shameful, wicked, abominable law and I'll break it, for one, the first time I get a chance") to the daring slave Eliza who braved the river's ice to rescue her son from being sold away from her.

Despite an overwhelmingly positive reception, the book had detractors. It was criticized as being overly romantic and melodramatic, and as being based purely on fiction. Southern readers accused Harriet of being ignorant of the real world of slavery. She was even criticized for speaking on such indelicate subjects as the sexual exploitation of slave women by their white masters.

Such criticism prompted her to compose in 1853 the *Key to Uncle Tom's Cabin,* in which she listed for her detractors "all the original facts, anecdotes and documents on which the story is founded." Harriet found this book even harder to write than *Uncle Tom's Cabin,* since it listed in chilling detail direct evidence of abuse of slaves. She also noted that she could not even tell all the truth about slavery in *Uncle Tom's Cabin,* since it would be too terrible for many to read, that "slavery in some of its workings, is too dreadful for the purposes of art."

In 1853, with the *Key* finished, Harriet and Calvin set off for England and Scotland to meet with anti-slavery societies. *Uncle Tom's Cabin* was selling well in England, and wherever Harriet and her group traveled she was cheered and feted and given money to help with "the cause." She was introduced to such literary notables as Charles Dickens and William Thackeray and was showered with gifts, including a gold chain bracelet inscribed with the dates of the abolition of the slave trade in England. In 1865 she was able to inscribe a similar message on other links of the chain when the Thirteenth Amendment to the Constitution finally abolished slavery in the United States once and for all. In 1856 she published *Dred,* which would be her last anti-slavery novel.

In 1857 she and Calvin suffered a terrible blow when their son Henry drowned while swimming in the Connecticut River. To deal with her grief Harriet began almost immediately to write *A Minister's Wooing*, a romantic novel of a sailor who drowned at sea, a dramatic change for her.

When the Civil War finally came on April 12, 1861, her son Fred enlisted, as did several of her nephews. Harriet and her family watched and waited as the war progressed, becoming increasingly impatient with President Lincoln and his hesitancy to free the slaves. Harriet felt strongly that the war was punishment for the nation's sin of slavery and that only through abolition of that institution could the nation survive. But she was forced to be patient. As much as he respected her work, President Lincoln had his own plans for the war and would not be rushed.

Finally, on December 2, 1862, Harriet was invited to visit the White House. Her daughter Harriet, her son Charley, and her sister Isabella—a noted suffragist—accompanied her. According to Beecher legend, the tall, lanky President Lincoln rose from his chair and greeted Harriet with the statement, "So you're the little woman who wrote the book that started this great war." Legend also has it that he assured Harriet that he would issue the Emancipation Proclamation very soon. When it was indeed issued on January 1, 1863, Harriet felt her years of writing and protest had finally borne fruit.

Later years would see the Stowes move to Hartford, first to an enormous and expensive house call Oakholm, and later to a more modest home in the Nook Farm section of Hartford. Harriet also bought an orange grove in Florida where she and Calvin spent the winter months. She continued to write and to support her family with her writings. She died in Hartford on July 1, 1896.

Harriet Beecher Stowe lived at a time when women's voices were muted by both custom and law. They were not allowed to speak in public, nor were they allowed to vote. The only sanctioned means of protest available to them was the pen, and Harriet used hers mightily to galvanize public opinion against what she considered to be her nation's greatest sin. Lyman Beecher had always prized sons because they could preach his religious message to the world. But his daughter's words would live longer and would be heard by millions more people than his sons' would ever be. In a family of preachers, hers would be the sermon that the world would never forget.

CAROLINE MARIA HEWINS

1846–1926

Pioneer in Library Services
for Children

*T*he children were everywhere. They perched on chairs and sprawled over tables, their books open and spread out before them. They occupied virtually every available seat in the room, their legs dangling from the seats of the chairs. A photograph of the scene published in the local newspaper showed two adults and no fewer than fifty-one children in the room, all quietly and seriously absorbed in their reading. It looked a typical Sunday afternoon in any children's room in any library in the land.

Except this was not a children's room—it was the main reading room of the Hartford Public Library, and in 1904 it was used by both adults and children. To the despair of the library's director, Caroline Maria Hewins, there was no separate children's room, and despite the differences in temperament and reading materials, both children and adults were forced to use the same limited space.

For years Caroline Maria Hewins had implored the library's board of trustees to allow her to establish a separate space for the

Caroline Maria Hewins

many children who used the library regularly, and to develop a collection that would suit their specific needs and tastes. But her pleas had fallen on deaf ears—until the day the local paper published the telling photograph. Within the next few months the library was able to secure the use of three bright, sunny rooms in a house adjacent to the main building. After twenty-nine years as the administrator of the library, Caroline Maria Hewins's dream of a children's room in the library was about to come true.

Knowing her passion for children's services, the board of trustees might have suspected that the photographer from the local paper had not simply happened by that Sunday afternoon. They might have also guessed that those fifty-one children had not just wandered in, although many children often did. That Sunday they had been invited to visit by the director and had been asked to be waiting at the door when the library opened at two in the afternoon. But for Caroline Maria Hewins such subterfuge was both warranted and excusable. She believed the children's needs were paramount; they had waited long enough. If the board of trustees needed a gentle reminder of this, and that reminder appeared in the local paper, she would be more than happy to take the credit or the blame for it.

Caroline Maria Hewins had taken risks before. At a time when it was rare for a woman to work outside the home, she served as director of the Hartford Public Library, a position she would hold for fifty years. She opened the library on Sundays to serve the working people of Hartford. She established branches throughout the area in schools, settlement houses, and factories. But it was her establishment and promotion of library services for children that became her most enduring legacy.

Caroline's own childhood had been steeped in the love of nature, literature, and the magic of the written word and had prepared her perfectly for her chosen profession. She was born in

Roxbury, Massachusetts, in 1846, the oldest of nine children of Charles Amasa and Caroline Chapin Hewins. When she was seven years old her family moved to West Roxbury, to a large house surrounded by five acres of land planted with flowering trees and shrubs, and a vegetable garden that "gave all that we could use and some for friends." Her parents both loved gardening and instilled in all their children a love of nature and the out-of-doors. There was a little pond filled year-round with goldfish and a rolling pasture that was home to a cow named Jessie. Her father was a successful businessman who traveled frequently, but the household was never lonely while he was gone; besides the parents and nine children it was home to a great-grandmother, grandmother, uncle, and two aunts.

Growing up in a rural community, the children enjoyed traveling magic shows, dance parties, and walks in the woods to pick wild huckleberries in the summer and apples in the fall. It was not the out-of-doors though that brought Caroline the most pleasure throughout her childhood but the enriching and sometimes exotic world she found between the covers of the books in the family library.

She learned to read by the age of four, taught first at home by her mother and later in a local private school. The world she discovered in books offered her a kaleidoscope of experiences— everything from friendship and wild adventure to reassuring comfort on a stormy Sunday afternoon. The first book she ever owned was entitled *Lucy's Conversations*, by Jacob Abbot and after mastering that she quickly moved to reading *Aesop's Fables, Robinson Crusoe*, and a great favorite, *The Swiss Family Robinson*. At the age of seven she had read *Uncle Tom's Cabin* so many times she could almost recite it by heart. She loved the challenge of puzzles, clever rhymes, and the music of poetry.

She read Washington Irving's *Sleepy Hollow* and reported on her delightful discovery of that author in her autobiography, *A Mid-Century Child and Her Books:* "One day there was a thunder shower, and as I did not enjoy being kept in a room with shut windows and preferred standing at an open door, I was beguiled into forgetfulness of heat and lack of oxygen by the offer of Irving from the grown-up bookcase. It was the double-columned volume that opened *The Alhambra,* the gate with the hand holding the key, the magic tower, the mimic battle, the Arabian astrologer and the Christian maiden down, down in the caverns. I never stopped to ask if the words were long or the style was prolix, but read, read, read until the sky was clear and the sun shone."

By the age of fifteen she had an "intimate acquaintance" with such authors as Charles Dickens, Sir Walter Scott, William Thackeray, Alfred Lord Tennyson, and Henry Wadsworth Longfellow, and a slight flirtation with William Shakespeare. The family's subscriptions to the popular magazines of the day offered further entertainment—*Harper's Magazine,* with its biographical sketches and enthralling ghost stories, and *Godey's Lady's Book,* filled with poems and stories by well-known authors of the day, including her old favorite, Washington Irving. Exposure to the art world came from her grandfather, Amasa Hewins, a portrait painter in Boston. The *London Art Journals* were a staple in the family library and offered the whole family a wonderful diversion on Sunday afternoons.

The West Roxbury library was located in a small room in a local hall. It was tended by an elderly couple and kept alive by subscriptions of a dollar a year. In her last year in the local school Caroline served as the secretary of the library association and worked in the library when the elderly couple was away. She experienced a real flush of pleasure when she discovered she knew the collection well enough to help others find rewarding reading material.

After graduation from Eliot High School in 1862, she attended the Girl's High and Normal School of Boston to prepare for a teaching career since, with few professions open to women, teaching seemed a logical choice. The headmaster of her school sent her one day on a project to the Boston Athenaeum, a private research library. But when the project was finished, she had so fallen in love with the library, with the many books and the "air of quiet and leisurely study," that she was loath to leave and—in a moment of brave enthusiasm—asked the head librarian, William Frederick Poole, for a job. She was hired a few weeks later.

William Frederick Poole was already famous in library circles for his publication in 1848 of *Poole's Index to Periodical Literature. Poole's* became one of the classic reference works in libraries and was later replaced by the *Reader's Guide to Periodical Literature,* which is still in use today. William Frederick Poole was a champion of libraries and a strong believer in the librarian as a professional. Caroline learned the rudiments of sound bibliographic practice under Poole— knowledge that would serve her well in the future. After a year under his tutelage she had no doubts that she had found her life's work. In 1875 she accepted a position as the librarian in the Hartford Young Men's Institute, another private, subscription library. She began managing the Institute almost immediately.

Remembering a childhood spent in the company of imaginative books, she was appalled to discover there were few books at all for children in the collection, and those paltry few were shelved inappropriately with the adult books. Caroline disposed of those books she thought unsuitable, those "full of profanity and brutal vulgarity," and chose those she thought were more appropriate. Many of the books she purchased were those she herself had enjoyed as a child. She invited the members' children to visit the library and consulted them on what they liked to read.

Caroline Maria Hewins's beginning career as a librarian would be marked by a time of sweeping change in libraries throughout the United States. *The Report on Public Libraries in the United States of Amer-*

ica by the Department of the Interior, Bureau of Education, published in 1876, stated there were then 3,682 libraries throughout the United States, but only 290 (fewer than 10 percent) reported that they were free, public libraries. Many were medical or academic libraries or libraries that charged a fee or subscription, as did the Hartford Young Men's Institute. Throughout the library systems there was a glaring scarcity of services designed especially for children. Many public libraries barred children younger than twelve or fourteen from using the library at all!

But times were changing. In 1876 the American Library Association (ALA) was organized, with its main goal being to promote library service to the public, and to promote the idea of the librarian as a professional. The ALA began monthly publication of the *American Library Journal* in 1876, and that same year Melvil Dewey of the Amherst College Library described a uniform system of cataloging books that would become the Dewey Decimal System. Libraries were being considered as auxiliaries to public education, which was already receiving the benefit of tax dollars and becoming freely available to all children. The next logical step was to expand public library services for children as well.

The 1876 *Report* by the Department of the Interior was decidedly in favor of such a move. In its chapter "Public Libraries and the Young," author and librarian William I. Fletcher asserted, "Who will presume to set the age at which a child may first be stirred with the beginnings of a healthy intellectual appetite on getting the taste of a strong meat of good literature? This point is of the first importance. . . . If there is any truth in the idea that the public library is not merely a storehouse for the supply of the wants of the reading public, but also and especially an educational institution which shall create wants where they do not exist, then the library ought to bring its influences to bear on the young as early as possible."

Caroline could not have agreed more. She shared Fletcher's view that the public library had a responsibility to provide both children and adults with quality reading material. But who would choose these materials, and who would decide what was "good," especially for children? Fletcher again echoed her beliefs exactly when he wrote, "Good juvenile books must have something positively good about them. They should be not merely amusing or entertaining and harmless, but instructive and stimulating to the better nature. . . . The 'better books' should be duplicated so as to be on hand when called for; these should be provided in such numbers merely that they can occasionally be had as the 'seasoning' in a course of good reading." Fletcher also believed, as many did, that the public library should exist as an adjunct of the public school system and suggested the libraries and schools work together to develop reading programs and materials for youngsters that would complement their formal studies.

There were almost no book lists of appropriate titles for children available, so Caroline began composing her own. In 1878 the Hartford Young Men's Institute began to issue a quarterly bulletin. She found this offered a perfect opportunity to include suggestions of quality reading materials for boys and girls and offered to "gladly cooperate with fathers and mothers in the choice of children's books." In 1882 Caroline published the first of her noteworthy bibliographies, *Books for the Young, A Guide for Parents and Children.*

Books for the Young was the first list of its kind and had been compiled at the request of Frederick Leypoldt, then editor of *Publishers' Weekly.* In the introduction to *Books for the Young* Caroline advised parents to read to their children and to not let the children read anything the parents had not read themselves. "Give children something that they are growing up to," she counseled, "not away from, and keep down their stock of children's books to the very best."

In 1878 the Hartford Young Men's Institute became the Hartford Library Association. In 1892 it became a free library and in 1893 it moved to larger quarters and was finally renamed the Hartford Public Library. The population of the city exceeded 45,000 people at that time, and the demand for library services was growing. Even without separate facilities for children, the Hartford Public Library circulated 50,000 children's books during its first year as a public entity, 25 percent of its entire circulation.

Caroline opened a branch of the library in one of the local settlement houses and worked there herself for one hour each evening. (She ultimately felt so comfortable there that she made it her own home for twelve years.) She established a branch of the Agassiz Association (named for the famed naturalist Louis Agassiz) in the library and conducted nature walks on Saturday mornings, leading the children in a search for birds, insects, and wildflowers. On inclement days there were readings from the works of such nature authors as John Burroughs and Henry David Thoreau.

Caroline tried to inspire the children with a love of the classics and read aloud to them from the works of Dickens, Thackeray, and Scott. Youngsters were enthralled by tales of knights and dragons and were introduced to *Pilgrims Progress* and *Don Quixote*. They were encouraged to join in book discussions and to act out their favorite scenes in small theatricals. In 1904 her dream for a children's room finally became a reality, and two years later the Hartford Public Library was finally able to hire a full-time children's librarian.

The hiring of the children's librarian freed Caroline to expand her influence both throughout the state and on a national level. In a profession that was still dominated by men, she forged a path for women, becoming the first woman to speak at an ALA conference and the first women to hold a seat on its board of directors. She helped found the American Library Association's Children's Division, the Education Association (a forerunner of the PTA), and the Connecticut Library Association, where she served as president from 1912 to 1913. She was instrumental in the creation of the Public Library Committee in Connecticut in 1893 and traveled tirelessly throughout the state, sometimes by horse and buggy, to plead for the establishment of local libraries and, of course, the purchase of good books for children.

She regularly contributed articles to *Library Journal* and other publications and lectured in the newly established library schools. In 1911 Trinity College of Hartford awarded her an honorary master's degree in recognition of her distinguished services to the City of Hartford and her position as an educator, the first woman to be so honored.

Caroline loved to travel, but even on trips abroad she did not forget "her" children, and she wrote lively and informative letters to them. Eventually these took the form of a column titled "A Traveler's Letters to Boys and Girls" and published in the *Hartford Courant*, in which she wrote that, try as she might, she simply "couldn't get away from her children and books." The columns were later published in a book of the same name. In 1926 she published a record of her own childhood readings in the autobiographical *A Mid-Century Child and Her Books*, which still offers delightful insight into the basis of her practices as a librarian

Caroline found time to act as mentor to others entering the field of children's library services which, from its beginning, was dominated by women. At a time when there were few professions open to women besides teaching, the job of children's librarian offered a unique entry into a respected, growing profession. Children's librarians were primarily young, educated, and energetic women from homes of above-average income. They brought to the profession a singular dedication to the service of the young.

Caroline's primary protégé and good friend Anne Carroll Moore would go on to manage the children's room at the New York Public Library for thirty-five years, from 1906 until 1941. Caroline Maria Hewins and Anne Carroll Moore became undisputed leaders in the field, bringing their influence to bear not just on other librarians but on writers, publishers, and editors—the whole field of children's literature and library services. They would shape the profession and in turn be shaped by its spontaneous and successful evolution.

Caroline was still working in 1925 when she celebrated her fiftieth anniversary as the director of the Hartford Public Library. In commemoration of her anniversary, friends and fellow librarians offered her the sum of $7,000 and asked her to choose between taking a trip to Europe or endowing a scholarship for librarian studies in her name. It was no surprise to those friends that she chose the scholarship. Explaining why she did not choose Europe, she told her good friend Anne Carroll Moore, "I can always get there somehow when I feel I must. A scholarship will last longer and it will be such fun to find the right girls for it."

Unfortunately, Caroline did not live long enough to choose such girls. She died on November 4, 1926, after a trip to visit Anne Carroll Moore at the New York City Public Library. She was eighty years old. Caroline was described as a "typical New England school-teacher in figure, speech and manner" and enjoyed a wide circle of friends who enjoyed her loyalty and keen sense of humor. She lived a modest, frugal life, consumed by her work. She never married and never retired.

Caroline Maria Hewins entered the library field with no mentors, no guideposts, no charted course to follow. She had little formal preparation, but very high standards. She made up her own rules and followed her own instincts. In the fifty-one years of her service she witnessed impressive change in the field and effected much of it herself—the establishment of the public library as an important community institution and cultural center, the emergence of the librarian as a respected professional, and the development of special services for children. In 1875 children were often not welcomed in libraries. Today the children's room is automatically accepted as an integral and vital part of every public library in the land.

Caroline Maria Hewins loved and respected children and had confidence in their opinions. She did not dismiss them as insignificant small people who should be "seen and not heard" but instead saw them as a group whose opinions and desires should be listened to and respected. She believed firmly that the gift of good books and reading would lead to an intellectual development in the young that would offer a fuller and more rewarding life. This was her life's work, and she brought all her energies to bear on its success. In 1951 *Library Journal* named her to its Library Hall of Fame.

The Hartford Public Library still offers the Hewins Scholarship of $4,000 annually for the study of library science, specifically in children's services. Caroline Maria Hewins's influence is still remembered and respected in public libraries throughout America.

MARTHA MINERVA FRANKLIN

1870–1968

Champion of Black Nurses

*T*hey had come a long way, that small band of black women climbing the White House steps. They had traveled from the teeming streets of crowded American cities and from the quiet country lanes of rural villages throughout the nation, leaving families, patients, and colleagues behind, a constituency that would be hard pressed to cope without them.

But they would be home soon enough to take up their burden of responsibilities. Today they would savor a small moment of triumph. For in less than sixty years their race had traveled from the degradations of slavery to the status of respected members of society, invited to visit the seat of American power at a reception with none other than the president of the United States and his wife. Carrying a large basket of American Beauty roses, they entered the White House, taking one more step in their continuing and tumultuous journey toward equality.

It was 1921 and the women were members of the National Association of Colored Graduate Nurses (NACGN). At a convention meeting in Washington, D.C., the members visited the White House to deliver the message to President Warren Harding

Martha Minerva Franklin, 1908

that their group of thousands of trained black nurses was ready to offer their services anywhere in the world, whenever and wherever needed.

For Martha Minerva Franklin it must have been a bittersweet moment, since this was to be her last convention. The NACGN had been her brain child, a dream that she had finally seen realized in August 1908 when fifty-two black nurses had joined her in New York City to consider the need to form a viable national organization for nurses of their race. Martha and her colleagues lived and worked in a world where racial bias affected both their personal and professional lives, a world where discrimination against blacks was a daily and lifelong companion. By organizing into a national and cohesive unit, they sought dignity and respect for their race, their gender, and their profession.

Others would join them along the way: Adah B. Thoms, who would later work to see black nurses admitted to the American Red Cross and the U.S. Army Nurse Corps. Lillian Wald, founder of the Visiting Nurse Society and the Henry Street Settlement House in New York City's lower east side, would be the first white nursing leader to offer the group invaluable encouragement and support. Mary Eliza Mahoney, the first black professional nurse in America, would act as an inspiration to them all. But it was Martha Minerva Franklin who had the courage and foresight to take the first step.

Martha was born on October 29, 1870, to a black working-class family in New Milford, Connecticut, the second of three children. Her father, Henry J. Franklin, was a laborer who had fought in the Civil War. Her mother was Mary E. Gauson. The family later moved to Meriden, Connecticut, where Martha attended public schools, graduating from high school in 1890. In 1895 she was accepted into the Women's Hospital Training School of Philadelphia.

The Women's Hospital Training School of Philadelphia was founded by Ann Preston, a graduate of the Philadelphia Female

Medical College. After graduation Ann had remained with the College as a faculty member and later became dean, the first woman dean of any medical school. Ann Preston was a Quaker whose family had been ardent participants in the abolition movement, and who believed firmly in equal rights for women. Because women usually encountered difficulties when trying to enter the medical profession, the aim of the Women's Hospital Training School of Philadelphia (founded in 1862) and its School for Nurses (founded in 1863) was to make a medical education more accessible to women, both as doctors and as nurses. One of its strict rules was that the chief resident of the hospital must be a woman. Martha was only the second black to attend the nursing school, and when she graduated two years later in 1897, she was the only black woman in her graduating class.

Martha was entering the nursing profession at a time when the medical field was experiencing what would be lasting and profound changes. The last decade of the nineteenth and the first decade of the twentieth century witnessed a proliferation in the number of hospitals established throughout the country. As more advanced clinical and scientific techniques in medicine and surgery were developed, the public's perception of hospitals gradually evolved from being a place where you went to die to a place where you might go to seek a cure. And as the evolution of modern medical practices fueled a demand for hospital services, the need for trained nurses grew as well.

The idea of a professionally trained nurse was a relatively new one; the first schools had only opened in the late-nineteenth century. Massachusetts General Hospital in Boston opened a school in 1873; Bellevue Hospital in New York City followed soon after. Until then nursing had been considered a noble calling for women, but one that depended primarily upon the "feminine" characteristics of self-sacrifice, motherly devotion, and physical care. It was not considered a field in which women needed to be formally trained. But as the end of the nineteenth century approached, not only was the hospital movement growing but the movement seeking advanced educational opportunities for women was growing as well. As more women entered institutions of higher learning and joined more professions, nursing presented itself as a profession in which women might assume new and important positions.

The role of nurse was certainly not a new one for black women—traditionally black women had always provided health care to their people, including the nurses and midwives who practiced on the plantations of the South. These early practitioners were responsible for the treatment of illnesses and pregnancies of both blacks and whites on the plantations and used a combination of methods that might include herbal remedies carried over from their home country of Africa, astute powers of observation, and trial and error. Such early nurse-practitioners were almost always formally uneducated. As the nursing profession grew it presented a possibility for black women as well as white women to become educated and to enter a profession that would provide an honorable and lucrative living.

Attendance of a black woman at a predominantly white nursing school was almost an anomaly at the end of the nineteenth century, however. Most of the hospital nursing schools in the North imposed racial quotas, and many schools in the South excluded black women entirely, an exclusion that forced them to open and maintain their own schools. The scarcity of nursing schools that would accept black women went hand-in-hand with the poor quality of health care available to blacks in general.

Blacks often lived in abject poverty, in disease-ridden ghettos deep within crowded cities. Responding to the fear that the infectious diseases that blacks suffered from, including tuberculosis, would eventually affect the white population, white philanthropists endowed numerous hospital and working schools for black nurses; however, black women were still denied access to the more technically advanced schools white women attended. John D. Rockefeller and his wife Laura Spelman Rockefeller endowed the first college for black women in the country, the Atlanta Baptist Female Seminary in 1881, adding a department of nursing in 1886, a two-year program that led to a diploma. The school was later renamed Spelman College. Other schools soon followed, including the Freedman's Hospital Nursing School in 1894, later affiliated with Howard University of Washington, D.C.

Although some of the schools for black nurses endowed by white philanthropists offered an excellent education, most schools for blacks were poorly financed. Students were forced to study in dilapidated classrooms, where they suffered from lack of trained teachers and inadequate supplies. The schools were often attached to hospitals that served only black patients; thus students were hampered by limited training and inferior patient care. Black nurses also discovered that after training their employment opportunities were severely limited, as most white hospitals would not employ them, and those that did usually limited their assignments to caring for black patients only.

After graduation in 1897 Martha moved to New Haven, Connecticut, and began her professional career in private duty nursing, since black nurses were seldom employed in hospitals or as public health nurses. Such employment was isolating, however, and within the next few years Martha began to take notice of other limitations the color of her skin imposed. Not only did black nurses experience prejudice in regard to hiring practices and salary structure, but they were also mostly prohibited from membership in national organizations. Such membership played an important role for nurses, as it facilitated communication with others in their profession and helped them keep abreast of developments in the medical field. When the American Nurses Association (ANA) was formed in 1896, it limited membership to those who belonged to state organizations, many of whom disallowed blacks, or to alumnae of white nursing schools, thus preventing almost all black nurses from joining. Those few who qualified were not encouraged to join.

Martha became convinced that a national organization for black nurses was the answer to their needs. Such an organization could promote higher professional standards, encourage black nurses to seek leadership positions within the profession, and more clearly illustrate to the medical community the value of black nurses. But first she needed to determine if there was indeed an interest in forming such an organization.

To this end she began a letter-writing campaign that would take two years and absorb much of her free time and not a small amount of her personal finances. First she sent hundreds of letters to superintendents of nursing schools, representatives of nursing organizations, and professional graduate nurses. On the basis of this preliminary survey, Martha was able to discern an active interest in a national organization in many of her black colleagues. She then sent another 1,500 letters to those colleagues asking them if they would be interested in attending a national gathering.

The establishment of a national organization caught the interest of Adah B. Samuels (Thoms), president of the Alumnae Association of Lincoln Hospital School of Nursing in New York City. Adah was a staunch advocate of her fellow black nurses and worked tirelessly for their continued advancement. After graduating from Lincoln Hospital School of Nursing, Adah served there as assistant superintendent of nurses for eighteen years, later breaking the color barrier by becoming one of the first black acting directors. Like Martha, Adah was convinced that a national organization of black nurses would further the cause of the black nurse on many fronts. She invited Martha to convene a meeting in New York City under the sponsorship of the Alumnae Association of Lincoln Hospital School of Nursing

The first meeting of the National Association of Colored Graduate Nurses (NACGN) convened on August 25, 1908, when fifty-two black nurses met at St. Mark's A.M.E. Church in New York City. A prayer was offered by the Reverend W. H. Brooks, and Adah B. Samuels (Thoms) delivered an address of welcome. Martha was unanimously elected as the group's first president.

The minutes of the organization, housed at the Shomburg Center for Research in Black Culture in New York City, offer fascinating insight into the workings of the group. From the very beginning, it was run on a strictly professional basis: detailed minutes were kept, dues were collected, reports were made. Informative papers were read and discussed; one of the first was a paper read on the Colored Visiting Nurse Association of Philadelphia. At that historic first meeting committees were formed to "frame the objective of the convention," and the registration of nurses began. Nurses came from Pennsylvania, Washington, D.C., Virginia, Georgia, New York, and North Carolina. While all black nurses were to be accepted, full membership was reserved for registered nurses who had completed a three-year course at a school associated with a hospital. Twenty-six nurses were listed as charter members of the group.

The following year the group met in Boston, Massachusetts, where Martha was unanimously elected president for a second year. When she refused the appointment for a third term, the membership designated her as honorary president for life. At that meeting the NACGN was further bolstered by the attendance—and introduction to the group—of Mary Eliza Mahoney.

Mary Eliza Mahoney had been born in 1845 in Roxbury, Massachusetts. As a young girl she had exhibited a strong interest in becoming a trained nurse, but it would be many years before she would realize that goal. When she was eighteen years old she accepted a job at the New England Hospital for Women and Children as a cook, cleaning woman, and laundress—a job she worked at for fifteen years. Finally, at the age of thirty-three, she was admitted to that school as a student nurse. She graduated in 1879, thus becoming the first black professional nurse in the United States.

Mary registered with the Nurses Directory at the Medical Library in Boston and soon found work as a private duty nurse. Her competence and diligence became well known and she worked steadily at her profession. But she could not escape the fact that black nurses were hampered professionally by racist policies of discrimination. When she learned of Martha's work to organize the NACGN, she joined heartily in the effort.

At the group's first official convention in Boston in 1909, Mary gave the welcoming address, beginning what would be a long and mutually rewarding relationship with the organization. In 1911 she, too, was awarded life membership and was also elected the national chaplain. She would continue to encourage black nurses to join the NACGN and to work for equal rights, both as nurses and as women. And she would establish a rewarding friendship with both Martha and Adah B. Thoms that would endure for many years to come. Together the three would define the goals of the organization, shape its progress from the original twenty-six charter members, and shepherd it to its eventual success.

As the organization grew it became obvious that it would need a central headquarters to conduct its business and to facilitate communication among its members. In 1918 office space was provided by the Young Women's Christian Association on 137th Street in New York City, and when that office closed, space was offered at the center of the National Health Circle for Colored

People. A national registry was established to place nurses in positions throughout the country. Finally, in 1934, the NACGN leadership voted to make that space its permanent location.

The NACGN was officially incorporated in the State of New York. The formal mission of the group was as follows:

> The purpose of this corporation shall be to promote the professional and education advancement of nurses in every proper way; to elevate the standard of nursing education; to establish and maintain a code of ethics among nurses; to own and control a permanent headquarters and all rights and property held by the National Association of Colored Graduate Nurses as a corporation duly incorporated under and by virtue of the laws of the State of New York.

Martha Minerva Franklin remained active in the NACGN, but as the years passed her name was mentioned less and less in the minutes. In 1921 she joined her fellow members at the historic visit to the White House to meet President Harding. The minutes of that meeting report that the President received them most cordially and gave each a "hearty handshake." But the NACGN members did not linger over their triumphant visit for long. The next day the session reconvened with a return to "business as usual."

Over the next thirty years the NACGN campaigned tirelessly to overcome racial bias, breaking down barriers one by one. It encouraged nursing schools to place black nurses in supervisory positions, noting that the practice of placing white nurses as administrators of black nursing schools was "unfair and discouraging to qualified Negro nurses who are eager to rise in their professional ranks." It continued to work to end discrimination in pay and benefits. Led by such forceful leaders as Adah B. Thoms and Mabel K. Staupers, it conducted campaigns to allow black nurses to serve in the military, which they were finally allowed to join during World War II.

Mabel K. Staupers had been born in the West Indies and had emigrated to New York as a young girl. After receiving her degree from Freedman's Hospital School of Nursing in 1917, she began working with black tuberculosis patients in Harlem. Staupers was appalled at the low quality of care given to most black patients, and with two black physicians helped to establish the Booker T. Washington Sanitarium in Harlem, where black patients could receive better quality care from their own black physicians.

In later years Mabel served as executive secretary of the NACGN. It was she who helped the NACGN realize a long-held goal of membership in the American Nurses Association when in 1948 the organization voted to permit black nurses to become members directly, eliminating the requirement that they must join through state organizations. By 1951 the NACGN felt it had achieved its major goals of breaking down racial bias against black nurses and took the unprecedented move of voting to disband.

So whatever became of Martha Minerva Franklin, the founder and first president of the NACGN? During the 1920s Martha had moved to New York City, where she enrolled in a postgraduate course at Lincoln Hospital, finally becoming a registered nurse. She found work as a school nurse in the New York City public school system. Not one to rest upon past successes, and possessed of a lifelong desire to continue learning, she enrolled in Teacher's College at Columbia University when she was fifty-eight years old. Later she attended classes at the Department of Practical Arts, later known as the Department of Nursing Education.

Martha never married. After retirement she moved back to Connecticut, where she lived with her sister Florence. She was deeply religious and was a member of the Dixwell Avenue Congregational United Church of Christ in New Haven. She died on September

26, 1968, at the age of ninety-seven and was buried in a family plot in the Walnut Grove Cemetery in Meriden, Connecticut. In 1976 Martha Minerva Franklin, Mary Eliza Mahoney, and Adah B. Samuels Thoms were all admitted posthumously to the Nursing Hall of Fame.

Because Martha had outlived all her family members, her name was not placed on the family gravestone. Years later this omission caught the attention of a volunteer at the Center for the Study of History in Nursing who was sifting through biographical information about outstanding nurses. As a result the Chi Eta Phi Sorority, Inc., a sorority of black nurses, arranged with an anonymous donor to have Martha's named etched on the stone. On June 13, 1998, a graveside ceremony was held honoring her achievements, and the Mayor of Meriden proclaimed that day as "Martha Minerva Franklin Day" in honor of her many years of dedicated service to both the nursing profession and the civil rights movement.

Martha Minerva Franklin saw the nursing profession move from a fledgling group of little more than untrained servants to a highly educated and respected profession of men and women of all races upon which the entire medical community depends. She did not simply seek equality for the black nurse in that profession, she insisted upon it, because she knew such equality was necessary to both personal and professional survival. She devoted many years of her life to an organization whose ultimate success led to its demise, a rewarding outcome that was due to her unflinching devotion and hard work.

MARY JOBE
AKELEY
1878–1966

World Explorer

*D*eath came unexpected and swift. To his companions the explorer's spirit had still seemed strong, his will to succeed at his mission still passionate, his heart still dedicated to the task at hand. Carl Akeley had returned to Africa—to that vast, unknown continent that in 1926 still throbbed with a primitive spirit unchecked by man—to take a small part back with him, to share its beauties with the outside world.

But it seemed Africa would have none of it. There in the Kivu District of the Belgian Congo, the home of the great gorilla, the place that Carl himself had proclaimed the most beautiful place in all the world, he fell ill and died. His widow watched in sorrow as the coffin of solid native mahogany was lowered into the grave in the volcanic rock, watched while the 5-inch-thick slab of cement sealed it closed. The future that had once seemed so bright with promise now seemed lost to her.

Mary Jobe Akeley had come to Africa with her husband to help him follow his dream. They were on an expedition to collect specimens—animals and plants—with which to create dioramas of

Mary Jobe Akeley

the African plain for the American Museum of Natural History in New York City. She had come along as a helper, but somewhere along the way his dream had become hers. She knew almost immediately that she would not leave that dream behind her, buried in a mountain of volcanic rock. Somehow, she decided, she would finish the job herself, with Carl's spirit beside her, urging her on "beyond any doubt or denial." Certainly no one was better suited to the task than she.

Mary Leonore Jobe was born on January 29, 1878, on a farm near Tappan, Ohio, the younger of two sisters. Her father was Richard Watson Jobe, whose family had immigrated in Colonial times from West England. Richard Jobe had fought in the Civil War, exhibiting at an early age the dual family traits of physical daring and patriotic fervor by enlisting in the service before his sixteenth birthday. Her mother was Sarah Jane Pittis, who had been born in Ohio and whose family had immigrated from the Isle of Wight and Hampshire in England. The Pittis family claimed several illustrious ancestors, including Thomas Pittis, who had been personal chaplain to King Charles II.

Growing up on the farm had both pleasures and trials for the young sisters. Mary walked 3 miles to school each day, on roads often flooded in the spring and frozen in the winter, and seldom missed a day. History and geography were her favorite subjects because she delighted in learning about faraway lands and strange peoples. Much of her childhood was spent in the out-of-doors, tramping through woods and across streams, with little time or inclination to indulge in the typical feminine pursuits of playing with dolls or "wearing petticoats." Such a hardy lifestyle developed in her both an endurance to bear physical discomfort and a thirst for adventure—an ache to "dream dreams" of travel far beyond the confines of her family's modest farm in rural Ohio.

Mary graduated from Scio College in Alliance, Ohio, in 1897, did graduate work at Bryn Mawr in Pennsylvania, and went on to receive a master's degree in history and English from Columbia University in New York City in 1909. Like many young educated women of her era, she spent time as a teacher, working for a year at Temple College in Philadelphia in 1902 and later joining the faculty of the Normal College of the City of New York, which later became Hunter College, where she remained on faculty until 1916.

But Mary did not spend all her time teaching. College friends introduced her to British Columbia, Canada, and she became enthralled with the region. Her spirit of adventure and love for the out-of-doors led her to continued exploration in the wilds of British Columbia, not an easy feat for a young woman in the early part of the twentieth century. Most young women her age were marrying, staying close to hearth and home. Instead, Mary was exploring—hiking rough trails, climbing mountains, canoeing down icy streams, and generally leaving most of life's physical comforts behind. After several initial expeditions to the area she was invited in 1909 by the Dominion Topographical Society to attempt a climb of Mount Sir Sanford in the Selkirk Mountains of British Columbia, a peak which she never reached, but which nonetheless offered her priceless experience in wilderness travel. It was on this expedition that Mary began her lifelong practice of recording her travels and adventures through ambitious photographic records. She also kept copious notes in small notebooks of her adventures, recording in poetic detail her joy in the beauties of the surrounding topography.

In 1913 she visited unexplored regions of northern British Columbia and southeastern Alaska on a trip that was sanctioned by the Hudson's Bay Company and the Canadian government, becoming one of the first white women to set foot in the region. Mary's goal was a study of the Gitskan and Carrier Indians of the region and to that end she traveled more than 800 miles, both on

foot and on horseback, visiting the Indians in their camps, studying their customs, and witnessing their ceremonies. In her corduroy
knickerbocker trousers and her high-laced hiking boots, she was a
wonder to the Indians, who could not believe a white woman had
trekked so far into the wilderness, backpacking her supplies and
enduring great physical hardship. So impressed were they with her
courage and stamina that they assumed the "Great Spirit had put
the soul of a man into her body," and thus they named her "Dene-
Sczaki," or "Man-Woman."

The following year she traveled to the Canadian Rockies to
attempt a climb on a mysterious and unnamed mountain peak
reported to be 200 miles northwest of Mount Robeson. Above
Mount Robeson lay uncharted territory, and Mary and her friend
Margaret Springate were anxious to be among the first to explore
and map the area. Mary reported in a magazine article about the
mission: " 'Why shouldn't we go in and have a look at that big
mountain?' Miss Springate and I had asked each other. . . . Here
was a chance to see what on the government maps was only a blank
white spot. Who knew, save a solitary Indian or two, what was hid-
den in the recesses of those dense forests and forbidden ranges?"

The women were tantalized by the thrill of the unknown and
by the excitement of doing "the individual thing which we ourselves
had chosen, and to do it because, in obtaining a bit or real knowledge hitherto unobtained, it gave unmeasurable satisfaction . . .
achievement for our own pure delight." They were accompanied by
several experienced guides, including Donald "Curlie" Phillips, who
had previously climbed Mount Robeson.

The trip lasted over six weeks and took the expedition by foot
and packhorse over the perilous terrain of fourteen mountain
ranges, through snowfields, and over glaciers. At one point the
horses could travel no farther and the expedition set off on foot,
the women carrying on their backs supply packs weighing fifteen

pounds. The party trudged through icy streams and scrambled over rock falls, finally catching view of the great white mountain that they had nicknamed Mount Kitchi and which was later named Mount Sir Alexander, its "ice-clad peak, its radiant towers . . . lovely beyond the portrayal of camera or pen."

Although the expedition was ultimately forced to turn back because of lack of food, it recorded important information of the region, and Mary was able to provide the Canadian government with a penciled map, including a map of the headwaters of the Fraser River. She returned to New York to lecture and write about her expeditions and in 1915 was elected a fellow of the Royal Geographical Society in London, one of the first women to be so honored.

In 1917 she returned to the region with Phillips for a winter expedition, undeterred by temperatures sometimes as low as -54 degrees. "My interest in this new and impressively beautiful country 'north of the 54' did not wane," she wrote. "Like all who find their greatest joy in the wilderness, I determined to return at my first opportunity and visit the area between the headwaters of the Fraser and the Peace." In 1925, in recognition of her contribution to the exploration of British Columbia, the Canadian government named a "fine peak, 11,000 feet in altitude" Mount Jobe in her name.

Mary's experience had taught her that women and girls could be comfortable in the outdoors—even in the wilderness—and, if encouraged, could develop the skills needed to live healthy and adventure-filled lives. To these ends she opened a camp for young girls on the banks of the Mystic River in Connecticut in the summer of 1916. Young women should learn about nature first hand, she asserted, and should be encouraged to achieve an ambitious level of physical fitness. At Camp Mystic the girls slept in tents named for mountain peaks in the Rockies and enjoyed the typical summer sports of swimming, hiking, horseback riding, and archery. Camp Mystic girls (including Mary, their director) all wore a uniform of middy blouses, scarves, and bloomers. They also learned about the culture of the Connecticut Native Americans, all under the watchful eye of their intrepid explorer-director. Camp Mystic enjoyed an outstanding reputation as a summer camp and attracted the daughters of wealthy and famous families, including two Hawaiian princesses. Tuition was $375 for the summer.

Mary invited successful explorers to visit and lecture at the camp, explorers such as Martin and Osa Johnson, who photographed African wildlife, and Vilhjalmur Stefannson, who was a famed Arctic explorer. Stefannson had a good friend who was an explorer in Africa and who had made four expeditions to the "Dark Continent." His name was Carl Akeley.

In addition to being a celebrated African explorer, Carl Akeley was a noted inventor and taxidermist. He had been to Africa four times, primarily to secure animals for natural history exhibits in various museums, taking innovative moving pictures of game with a camera he had invented himself. But his 1921 expedition had filled him with foreboding. In the five years from 1905 until 1910 he had noticed a marked reduction in the amount of wildlife on the African plains. Safaris had already become an organized business; some elephants were becoming wary of intruders. When he returned in 1921, he was concerned that if he did not act quickly to secure specimens for exhibits, there would be little game left to kill. Carl Akeley did not enjoy killing wildlife, but like his friend Theodore Roosevelt, he believed that if he did not bring specimens home to exhibit in the United States, the world would know nothing about game in Africa, and thus no one would be inclined to preserve it. The African Hall at the American Museum of Natural History, which was just in the planning stages, would help to preserve a "visual museum of untouched Africa" for the world.

Carl Akeley and Mary Jobe were almost instantly attracted to each other, despite the fact that Carl was still married but separated from his first wife, Delia Denning. Mary was a tall, athletic, and attractive brunette whose past exploits as an explorer of the Canadian Rockies probably added to her intrigue. After Carl's divorce from Delia became final, he and Mary were married in 1924.

Carl announced almost immediately that he expected Mary to give up her own pursuits and join him in his further explorations of Africa, and despite her heretofore independent life, Mary agreed. She was honored to be included in his life's work. In January 1926 the couple embarked on Carl's fifth and Mary's first expedition to Africa, an expedition that had two distinct goals. The first was to travel to what was then the Tanganyika Territory and Kenya to collect animals, plants, and other specimens to complete the African Hall at the American Museum of Natural History. The second was to visit the Parc National Albert in what was then the Belgian Congo (now the Democratic Republic of the Congo) to obtain plant and floral specimens to appear in the gorilla exhibit at the Museum of Natural History. The expedition was financed by George Eastman, of Eastman Kodak, and Daniel M. Pomeroy, partner of financier J. P. Morgan and trustee of the museum. Mary agreed to act as expedition secretary and safari manager.

From her first step onto Africa soil, Mary was thrilled and intrigued by the beauty that surrounded her. She arose in the early dawn to "meet the day more than half-way" and watch the mountains as they became drenched in glorious color by the brilliance of the rising sun. In her book *Carl Akeley's Africa* Mary wrote, "At sunrise and at sunset all the colors in the artist's palette run riot everywhere. . . . This is Africa, untouched, unmarred. Often for an hour after sunrise one near-by peak is decorated with a rosy pink cloud mass. At sunset its blue heights are draped in long flowing streamers of gold. As I write this I know it is impossible to convey more than the vaguest idea of the infinite beauty constantly saturating my soul."

Despite the beauty of their surroundings, the expedition faced great difficulties. The days were long and tedious. Mary suffered from malaria, the result of an intense attack by mosquitoes. Both Mary and Carl were exhausted by the long hours of intense labor—photographing animals during the day, hunting them in the late afternoon, and preparing the skeletons for preservation and shipping home in the evenings. They killed lions, wildebeest, wild dogs—not for killing's sake, but to create a realistic series of exhibits for the museum.

They photographed backdrops for the animal groupings and watched as the artists that accompanied the expedition recreated on canvas the sweep of plain, trees, and vegetation that would form the backdrop of the dioramas at the museum. Conditions were often difficult—they suffered from extreme heat, drenching thunderstorms, and marauding animals. Their vehicles often became mired in the muddy ruts of the washed-out roads.

Eventually Carl became ill and was forced to rest. Yet he insisted they travel on. The expedition wound its way from Tanganyika to what was then the Belgian Congo to complete the study of the mountain gorilla that Carl had begun in 1921. He also wanted to show Mary the area that he considered to be the most beautiful in the world, the place where he assured her "the fairies dance." But the trip proved to be too much for him. Soon after the expedition reached the Kivu District, Carl Akeley once again grew ill and on November 17, 1926, he died of fever and exhaustion.

Mary was stunned with grief. This was to be Carl's expedition, Carl's accomplishment. Now, suddenly, he was gone. She decided almost immediately that she had no choice but to continue his work and complete the goals of the expedition.

There was much still to be done—specimens to be collected,

cataloged, and preserved. They still needed a canvas painted for the gorilla exhibit, still needed topographical surveys completed, maps drawn, and scientific data gathered. For six weeks Mary toiled at an altitude of 12,000 feet, supervising the workers, photographing vegetation, and collecting specimens, all the while dealing with her own grief. The work was severely hampered by rain, sleet, cold, and heavy fog—weather that only reflected her mood. After a brief trip to Lake Hannington to photograph the famous flamingoes of the area, she finally returned to New York where the American Museum of Natural History named her special advisor for the development of the African Hall.

On May 19, 1936, the Akeley Hall of African Mammals was opened and dedicated in Carl's memory. A herd of African elephants greeted the visitors, as they still do today. The lifelike dioramas present realistic groupings of lions, koodoos, impala, and wild dogs, against painted backgrounds, accompanied by native plants and fauna.

For the rest of her life, Mary worked to preserve African wildlife, vegetation, and natives from what she feared was inevitable destruction. In 1925, at Carl Akeley's urging, King Albert had ordered the establishment of the Parc National in the Congo to protect the habitat of the mountain gorilla. In 1927 Mary was awarded the Cross of the Knight, Order of the Crown from King Albert in recognition of her work to help Carl achieve that goal.

In 1935 she returned to Africa to collect more plants for the exhibit. Just as she had studied the Carrier Indians in British Columbia, she now turned to the study of the customs and ceremonies of the Zulu and Swazi tribes. In 1947 she made her last trip to Africa to film and photograph the enlarged Parc National and to visit Carl's grave. Back home she continued to lecture, to raise funds for both the American Museum of Natural History and the protection of African wildlife from destruction. In 1931 she wrote in the *New York Times*, "Throughout the world primitive men and animals are making a last stand against the onslaught of the machine age. . . . Nowhere is this destruction more manifest than in Africa. That continent has long been famous for its great forests and plains and many strange animals. Today, however, the riches that made Africa a naturalist's paradise are endangered by the onward march of agriculture, commercial and industrial exploitation."

In addition to speaking engagements, Mary wrote prolifically. In 1929 she published *Carl Akeley's Africa, an Account of the Akeley-Eastman-Pomeroy African Hall Expedition of the American Museum of Natural History*. In 1945 she wrote *Rumble of a Distant Drum*, which provided further details of her journey to complete Carl's work. The book is written in the voice of a small Watusi boy who became her "Toto" and accompanied her everywhere. Through the boy's voice Mary's lyrical writing resonates with her devotion to African wildlife and her deep and abiding respect for the African people. In 1950 she wrote *Congo Eden*, which described her last trip to the Congo during which she continued to film the great African mammals, many of which were becoming increasingly rare.

Although the last years of her life were spent in the service of the preservation of African wildlife, she did return once in 1938 to British Columbia, on a "journey of rediscovery," to the land where she had first tasted the thrill of her own personal adventures. Mary then retired to her home in Mystic, Connecticut, where she died in 1966. Fortunately she never knew that Carl's grave, the place that she had always hoped would be a sanctuary in his memory, was vandalized and destroyed by poachers in 1979.

Mary Leonore Jobe was a respected explorer in her own right before she met Carl Akeley. But she recognized in him a kindred spirit. He offered her an opportunity to literally expand her horizons, to share a wonderful adventure with him, and she accepted gratefully. Gradually, through years of working together, she placed her own stamp upon the project, breathed her own adventurous spirit into it, until it became not just a fulfillment of his dream but of hers as well. It is entirely doubtful that the Akeley exhibit at the American Museum of Natural History would have ever been completed without her work.

Today the Akeley Hall of African Mammals still welcomes visitors to the American Museum of Natural History where Mary Jobe Akeley will always be known as the adventurous woman who "brought the African jungle to Central Park West."

KATHARINE HOUGHTON HEPBURN

1878–1951

Advocate of Suffrage and Birth Control

$\mathcal{T}$he young mother walked briskly, pushing the baby carriage through the park on a beautiful spring day in 1907. A red-haired infant daughter lay sleeping in the carriage, a two-year-old son toddled by his mother's side. To anyone who might be taking notice, they looked like any other well-dressed, prosperous little family out for their daily stroll.

But beneath the broadcloth jacket the young mother's heart was heavy, her thoughts clouded with frustration and an odd sense of unfulfilled longing. She was young and beautiful, married to a successful doctor, mother of two healthy children. She lived in a charming old house in the fashionable Nook Farm section of Hartford, Connecticut, with servants to assist her and a handsome husband who was devoted to them all. She should be grateful for her blessings, for her gracious, comfortable life. Why then was she so unhappy?

Katharine Houghton Hepburn had challenged the Victorian

Katharine Houghton Hepburn with (clockwise from lower left)
Katharine, Marion, Robert, Thomas, Richard, and Margaret

restrictions of both society and a tyrannical uncle for the right to attend Bryn Mawr College and to earn a degree. She prided herself on possessing an independent spirit that had led her to travel through Europe on her own and to earn her own money as a teacher. But like most young women in 1907, she discovered that when she married she was expected to leave that independent, professional life behind her and turn her attention to the exclusive care of her husband, children, and home. As much as she loved her present life, she could not help but ask herself the question so many young educated women have asked, "Is this all I am here for?"

Her mother's dying wish had been that she and her sisters become educated so they could live independent, socially useful lives. The three girls had willingly embraced their mother's dream and had taken it as their own. But where was the dream now? Now that she was married and a mother, had those hard-won battles for personal fulfillment and independence been just that—only a dream?

It would be two years before she would find at least a partial answer to that question. She would calm some of her restlessness during those years by helping her husband wage a battle against the evils of venereal disease and by joining other prominent women in Hartford in an active campaign to close the houses of prostitution in the city. But her life would finally change dramatically one day in 1909 when her husband came home with some exciting news. Emmeline Pankhurst, the famous suffragist from England and founder of the Woman's Social and Political Union, was visiting Hartford and would speak that night. "Do you want to attend?" her husband, Tom, asked. Indeed she did! More than 200 women joined her at the meeting to listen to the British suffragist exhort them to fight for the most powerful political weapon of all, and the one they still did not possess—the right to vote. With her good friend Emily Pierson at her side, Katharine listened to Mrs. Pankhurst's stirring rhetoric and knew she had found her cause. Her time of restless boredom was most definitely over.

Katharine Houghton was born on February 2, 1878, in West Hamburg, near Buffalo, New York. Her mother was Caroline Garlinghouse. Her father was Alfred Houghton, son of Amory Houghton Sr., who was the founder of the Corning Glass Works in Corning, New York. Two other daughters would join the family, Edith in 1879 and Marion in 1884. Alfred's first wife, Olive, had died in 1873 leaving him with an older daughter, Mary, who was half-sister to Katharine, Edith, and Marion. Though Mary lived with her grandmother, the half sisters kept in touch throughout their lives.

The family was at first happy and financially secure, living comfortably in West Hamburg. The girls swam in Lake Erie and bicycled along its shore. But Alfred was given to dangerous feelings of insecurity and to deep bouts of depression. In 1892, when Katharine was fourteen years old, he took his own life, leaving Caroline to bring up her three girls alone.

Caroline had always prided herself on an independent spirit, and after Alfred's death she was determined to avoid dependence on her wealthy and domineering brother-in-law Amory Houghton Jr. She was equally determined that all three of her girls would receive an education that would allow them to eventually support themselves and to lead independent lives. But scarcely two years later Caroline discovered she was dying of stomach cancer. She was terrified of leaving the girls and especially leaving them in the care of relatives who might not share her goals for them. Before she died on September 2, 1894, she made arrangements for all three to attend school in Bryn Mawr, Pennsylvania. Katharine would enter the college, and the two younger girls would attend a day school nearby. Edith was fourteen years old; Marion was eleven.

The sisters were devastated by their mother's death. As Caroline had feared, their uncle Amory objected strenuously to her last wish that the girls be educated. He tried to convince Katharine that higher education only made women coarse and unmannerly. Echoing a commonly held opinion of the day, he warned that too much study could tax a woman's brain and might even render her too ill to bear children. Worse, it would offer blatant evidence to society that her family could not support her and that she was studying for a degree because she would ultimately be forced to support herself. No self-respecting young man from a good family would marry her.

Katharine won her battle to attend Bryn Mawr only through persistent and skillful negotiations. She knew that at seventeen she would be old enough to appoint her own legal guardian and so threatened to choose someone Uncle Amory would not like. Amory was forced to agree to let the girls follow the wishes outlined in Caroline's will. After living briefly and unhappily with an uncle in Canandaigua, New York, the three girls moved to Bryn Mawr, where Katharine entered the university in October 1895.

Katharine was tall, dark-haired, and strong-willed. Once she achieved her mother's goal of getting into college she alternated between working hard and cramming for exams and exhibiting total disdain for studying or following rules. She was late to class. She defied regulations and rode horseback through the grounds of the school. She entertained friends in her rooms far into the night, consistently overspent her allowance, and even took up smoking a pipe.

But at Bryn Mawr she discovered that dedication to studies was prized and that when she worked hard she was treated with dignity and respect. Her behavior improved, and in 1900 she graduated with a bachelor's degree in chemistry, later attending graduate school at Radcliffe. Her sister Edith also graduated in 1900, thus fulfilling at least in part their mother's dying wish.

After years of striving for a goal, Katharine suddenly found herself without one. What would she do with the rest of her life? There were precious few professional opportunities available for young women in 1900 besides teaching or missionary work, neither of which appealed to her. Edith had been accepted to Johns Hopkins Medical School in Baltimore, but Katharine decided to see a bit of the world before "settling down."

Over Uncle Amory's strenuous objections, she sailed for Europe, arriving in Paris with a scant ten dollars in her purse. She convinced a generous bistro owner to rent her rooms on credit, promising him that her well-to-do family would reimburse him. She toured Europe for several months, haunted museums and libraries, even gambled at Monte Carlo, but was perpetually strapped for cash. She finally returned home to teach school near her sister Edith in Baltimore.

It was through Edith that Katharine met Thomas Norval Hepburn, Virginia-born son of a clergyman. Tom was a medical student studying at Johns Hopkins with Edith, and since their last names both began with "H" they were seated next to each other. He was tall and athletic with bright red hair and brilliant blue eyes, and Katharine was attracted to him immediately. "That's the one!" she told her sister Edith, and set out to convince him to marry her.

But Tom was not that easy to convince. He was ambitious, possessed a solid Victorian sense of morality, and would not be bullied into marriage. Both Katharine and Tom were headstrong and outspoken, both filled with restless ambition. They finally married in 1904 but had to conceal their marriage from the hospital where Tom worked as an intern, since interns were forbidden to marry.

Their first son, Thomas, was born in 1905. A daughter, Katharine, joined the family in 1907. Born with bright red hair,

Katharine would go on to become one of the most famous and successful stage and screen actresses of her time. When Tom entered private practice, the family purchased a large Victorian cottage in the Nook Farm district of Hartford. The Nook Farm community had long been home to writers and literary professionals, and in the previous century had boasted such famous residents as Harriet Beecher Stowe, author of the classic *Uncle Tom's Cabin,* and later Samuel Clemens, better known as Mark Twain. The Hepburns were at first warmly welcomed into the community and settled down to raise their family in their own charming, offbeat way. Four more children would eventually join the family, Richard in 1911, Robert in 1913, Marion in 1918, and Margaret in 1920.

The children were encouraged to excel in sports. They mastered handsprings and bold tumbling acrobatic stunts. They rode their bikes pell-mell through the leafy lanes of Nook Farm. In winter Tom hooked their sleds onto the back of the car and towed them through the snow-covered streets, with the children screaming and hanging on for dear life. In addition to physical daring they were encouraged to speak their minds, to ask questions, and to broach any subject—no matter how unorthodox or taboo. Katharine and Tom both believed in speaking frankly to their children about sex and reproduction, topics that were not usually openly discussed in the early part of the twentieth century. Katharine believed that if you were frank and open with your children, they would ultimately come to trust and confide in you.

As their family grew so did the couple's involvement in political and humanitarian causes. From the beginning of his career Tom Hepburn had led an active campaign to eradicate venereal disease. Through his medical practice he had seen first-hand the pain and suffering such disease brought, not just to men, but especially to innocent and unwitting young wives who suffered and died because of their husbands' infidelities. He and Katharine were both incensed by the presence of houses of prostitution in Hartford and worked closely with the mayor to have them closed. Tom helped to establish both the American Social Hygiene Association and the Connecticut Social Hygiene Association.

But it was the fight for suffrage that ultimately fired Katharine's spirit. After hearing Emmeline Pankhurst speak in 1909, she and her friend Emily Pierson came away energized and determined to organize an active suffrage campaign in their city and to revitalize the lagging movement in their state. They organized the Hartford Political Equality League, which later became the Hartford Equal Franchise League. The League attracted other enthusiastic young women who shared the passionate conviction that the time had finally come to win the battle for women's right to vote. Men had denied women political equality long enough.

Katharine had finally found a cause she loved, but she needed Tom's approval before she plunged head-on into such an absorbing job. The work was controversial. In 1909 it was unheard of for a woman in "polite society" to campaign for women's rights, or to discuss such contentious issues as birth control or venereal disease. She had already been warned by one of her neighbors that if she took up the suffrage cause "no one would have anything to do with you." Did Tom think such a controversial campaign would hurt his career? His reply must have reassured her that she had married the right man. "Of course it will, but do it anyway," he said. Tom believed firmly in "standing up for things you believe in." Katharine took him at his word. In 1910 she was elected president of the Connecticut Woman Suffrage Association and in 1911 became active in the movement to encourage the practice of birth control.

Katharine's concern that her activities would provoke the disapproval of the neighbors was well-founded, and she faced this challenge as she faced others in her life—head-on, resolutely. If a neighbor snubbed them, young Katharine remembered that her mother "continued to say good morning" until the other party was forced to respond. In the event they did not, Katharine assured her children that the other party obviously had not heard them. The Hepburns were fiercely devoted to one another and formed a unit that neighbors both disapproved of and envied. The actress Katharine Hepburn once stated fondly in a television interview, "My parents gave me the greatest gift anyone could give anyone—the freedom from fear."

Katharine included her children in her work, bringing them along to rallies and to march in suffrage parades and asking them to hand out balloons inscribed with the slogan "Votes for Women." The children were frequently included in lively discussions held in the Hepburn parlor with such famous visitors as Emmeline Pankhurst, activist Emma Goldman, and birth control advocate Margaret Sanger. From an early age they lived in a world where both men and women worked together to try to cure society's ills.

The typical women in Hartford who were drawn to the suffrage movement in the first decade of the twentieth century came from a cross-section of the population, but many were like Katharine Houghton Hepburn—white, middle class, well-educated, some from wealthy families. Many were unmarried and chose to remain that way. For some it was simply too difficult to try to combine marriage and family duties with working for the cause. In addition to their work to secure the vote, the women also campaigned to secure laws governing child labor. They lobbied for increased spending for hospitals and for improved recreational facilities for poor immigrants. And while there were fewer less affluent women working for suffrage, it would be a mistake to assume that poor women were indifferent. Many joined the movement in spirit but were hampered by their need to work or the dependence of large families on their time and resources.

Katharine threw herself into the work, serving as president of the Connecticut Woman Suffrage Association (CWSA) from 1910 to 1911 and again from 1913 to 1917. Under her leadership the group grew to a membership of more than 30,000 women. She distributed leaflets, wrote letters, and continually petitioned the legislature to pass laws favoring the protection of women and children. In between her terms as president she gave birth to two more boys, Richard in 1911 and Robert in 1913. But she became increasingly disenchanted with the more passive campaign of the CWSA and their sister association, the National American Woman Suffrage Association, claiming that their methods were hopelessly out of date. In 1917 she resigned her position as president to join the more militant organization founded by Alice Paul, the National Woman's Party.

Katharine was inspired by Alice Paul's single-minded devotion to the suffrage cause. She longed to go to Washington and join the picket lines. But in August 1919 she was pregnant again and felt it would be too dangerous. Instead, she paid the train fare for a young Irish secretary, Edna Mary Partell, to go in her place. Edna Partell was delighted to go. She was arrested several times and joined the hunger strike in the Old District Jail. She returned home to continue the fight for better conditions for working women.

The suffrage movement finally tasted sweet success in the spring of 1919 when Congress adopted the Nineteenth Amendment to the Constitution, stating, "the right of citizens of the United States to vote shall not be denied or abridged by the United States or by any State on account of sex." The amendment was ratified by the last needed state in August 1920. After more than seventy years of struggle, American women had finally won the right to vote. Katharine and other activists of the movement had worked hard and could take just pride in the realization of a long-held dream. Never one to mince words, Katharine was reported to have rejoiced that finally the legal status of women was raised to self-respecting adults and out of the class of "idiots, criminals and the insane."

In 1921 Katharine and Tom suffered a devastating blow when their oldest son, Tom, died under mysterious circumstances. Young Tom and his sister Katharine had been visiting an aunt in New York. On the morning they were planning to leave, his sister discovered Tom's body hanging by a torn piece of sheeting from a rafter in his upstairs room. It was immediately assumed that the young man had committed suicide, but both parents chose to reject that theory, surmising that he might have been attempting a daring stunt with the sheet, a stunt that had gone horribly wrong. The tragedy must have reminded the elder Katharine of the suicide of her own father many years before. The entire family was shattered by their loss, especially young Katharine, who had been close to her older brother.

In 1923, perhaps in an effort to assuage her grief at her son's death, Katharine formally joined with Margaret Sanger and other friends to form the Connecticut Birth Control League, which would later become Planned Parenthood of Connecticut. Katharine favored birth control for many reasons, not the least of which was her great respect for human life. She believed that every child should be a wanted child. And certainly poor women should have the same access to information about birth control as wealthier women, who had greater access to sympathetic physicians who could provide it for them. She deplored the stringent laws in Connecticut that prohibited the sale and distribution of birth control devices, in particular the Comstock Law, which was passed in 1873. The Comstock Law was named for Anthony Comstock, self-proclaimed public censor, who was instrumental in the passage of a federal obscenity statute that prohibited the transport of "obscene" literature via the public mails. Included in this ban was not just pornographic literature—"lewd, lascivious, filthy books, pamphlets and writings"—but also information about contraceptive devices and abortion. In addition, a Connecticut law dating from 1879 prohibited the use of contraception and also forbade physicians from prescribing its use. The Connecticut Birth Control League's chief goal was to work for repeal of the laws so that contraceptive advice and devices could be legally distributed in Connecticut to rich and poor alike.

Using skills in lobbying that she had honed during the suffrage campaign, Katharine testified repeatedly before Congressional committees, both in Washington and her home state of Connecticut, urging lawmakers to repeal the stringent laws she referred to as "the police-under-the-bed law." Opponents found it interesting that she would campaign so heavily for birth control when she herself had such a large family. It was obviously not children she was against but the lack of choice in the matter, especially for the poor. "Women want children," she reasoned, "but they want children they can properly take care of, children that they can afford, both physically and economically." She argued that birth control would "lead to more happy marriages and therefore to higher morality."

While she was actively involved with the birth control movement, her red-haired daughter Katharine was enjoying success in her acting career, a coincidence that Margaret Sanger would not have missed. It could not hurt the birth control movement when one Katharine Hepburn won an Academy Award for her performance in the film *Morning Glory* in 1934 while another Katharine Hepburn chaired the National Committee on Federal Legislation for Birth Control. It did worry Katharine that perhaps her daughter's career might be adversely affected by her mother's controversial activities.

In 1935, discouraged by the legislature's refusal to change the law, the Connecticut Birth Control League decided to go ahead and open a clinic in Hartford that would dispense birth control devices and advice to women. Despite fierce and vocal opposition from clergy of the Roman Catholic Church, the clinic stayed open for four years, dispensing services to needy women who wished to limit the size of their families.

But in 1940 numerous raids on the clinic, along with continued defeat of a change in the law, forced the closure of all the clinics in Connecticut. Incredibly, it would not be until 1965 that the historic *Griswold v. Connecticut* case finally resulted in the overturn by the U.S. Supreme Court of the eighty-six-year-old Comstock Law and the 1879 law. Not until 1965 was birth control information finally legally available in the State of Connecticut.

Sadly, Katharine Houghton Hepburn did not live to see this triumph. She died suddenly in her home in Hartford on March 18, 1951. She had spent the morning with her daughter reading the reviews young Katharine had received for her recent performance in a tour of *As You Like It*. She died quietly that afternoon.

Katharine Houghton Hepburn was born at a time when all women, rich or poor, were expected to conform to the strictures of a Victorian society. They were told their chief goals in life should be to marry and to have children, and to subjugate their own beliefs and desires to those of their husbands. To aspire to a career or education of one's own was to swim against the tide of public opinion. Katharine Houghton Hepburn took the advice of her mother, swam mightily against that tide, and taught her children, both sons and daughters, to do the same—to think for themselves and to stand up for what they believed in, no matter the cost.

The actress Katharine Hepburn, who died in June 2003, often credited her parents with her own courage to try new roles and to break new ground as an actress. "We felt our parents were the best two people in the world," she once told an interviewer, "and we were wildly lucky to be their children."

SOPHIE TUCKER

1884 (?)–1966

The Last of the Red Hot Mamas

*T*he young, blond singer paced nervously backstage, watching the stage door anxiously. The audience was slowly filling the seats at the Howard Atheneum Theater in Boston that afternoon in 1908, ready for a rousing vaudeville performance to begin. Soon it would be young Sophie Tucker's turn on stage, offering her a chance to perform that she could not afford to pass up. She had left husband, son, and parents back in Hartford, Connecticut, and had set out on her own to pursue a singing career in show business. She was finally working and getting paid to do what she loved. After this engagement she might even have a shot at a job with the successful Flo Ziegfeld, who had already given her a contract promising her one hundred dollars a week to appear in his *Ziegfeld Follies*. But now she feared she might see it all disappear in an instant, a budding and promising career over because of a mistake so trivial as a missing suitcase.

That suitcase held her costumes, but even more importantly it held her makeup. Sophie rarely appeared on stage without her makeup—makeup that turned her fair skin black and transformed

BILLY ROSE THEATRE COLLECTION, THE NEW YORK PUBLIC LIBRARY FOR THE PERFORMING ARTS, ASTOR, LENOX AND TILDEN FOUNDATIONS

Sophie Tucker

her from a young, Jewish, blond girl to a black-faced "coon shouter." Already there were signs all over Boston heralding the appearance of "Sophie Tucker, World Renowned Coon Shouter."

Without that disguise she would not be accepted on stage. Without that disguise her career might be over before it even got started.

Finally, the stage manager could wait no longer. This was vaudeville, after all, and there was an impatient and demanding audience waiting for the show to begin. Sophie would simply have to go on as she was or give up her spot on the program. Dressed in a simple tailored suit and her own fair skin, she slipped on stage. The audience was at first angry—they had been promised a glamorous black-faced singer, and here was a fair-skinned blond, dressed conservatively. But then she began to sing and when she had finished the crowd was on its feet, cheering and begging for more. She sang that night and the next day, and the audience loved her, just as she was.

When her suitcase arrived a few days later, the stage manager refused to let her go back to caking her face with black makeup and suggested she wear a long gown to add a little glamour to her act. So, in a borrowed gown and a tight corset Sophie Tucker stepped on stage to begin her career all over again, this time as no one but herself. For almost sixty years she entertained audiences with her own special combination of elegance, glamour, and brash, risqué theatrics, becoming one of the entertainment world's most spectacular and memorable personalities.

The story of Sophie Tucker's birth might easily have been written by a creative publicity agent anxious to provide his or her client with a story that would endear her to even the most hardened critic. But the tale of the poor, Jewish baby born in a stranger's farmhouse somewhere in Russia or Poland was all too true. Sophie's parents lived in a small Russian village at the end of the nineteenth century, during the waning days of Czar Alexander Alexandrovich's reign. Her father was a soldier in the Russian Army. Just before Sophie's birth he immigrated to the United States, seeking a better life for his family. He left his pregnant wife and two-year-old son Phillip behind, promising to send for them as soon as he was established in their new country.

Shortly before the baby's birth, Sophie's mother got a message from her husband telling her to join him in America, and so with Phillip in tow she began her journey. Traveling in a rickety horse cart, through dark and twisting country lanes, the frightened young woman soon found herself in labor and, to add to her horror, the driver suddenly abandoned her and her young son by the side of the road. Gathering her courage, she made her way to a nearby farmhouse where a kind couple took them in and where her first daughter was born; her mother was never very sure if Sophie was born in Russia or in Poland. (And we cannot be sure of the year of Sophie's birth—reported as anywhere from 1884 to 1887—since she may have lied about her age, as many performers did.)

Three months later the family was finally reunited in America where another surprise awaited them. Sophie's father, fearful of reprisals of the czar's army because of his defection, had taken on the identity of a traveling companion who had died on the journey. Instead of Kalish their name was now Abuza. The young Abuza family settled in Boston, Massachusetts, where two more children, another boy and girl, joined the family.

In 1892, when Sophie was eight years old, the family moved to Hartford, Connecticut, where her parents opened a kosher restaurant and delicatessen. To attract more customers her father declared that no meal in the restaurant would cost more than twenty-five cents. Diners could choose from a wide variety of kosher delicacies, including pickled herring, chopped liver, borscht (beet soup), noodle pudding, and potato kugel (soufflé or pudding). For another fifteen or twenty-five cents they could wash it down with whiskey, beer, or "soda pop." The restaurant soon became popular with residents of the Jewish communities in Hartford and was also a gathering place for the Yiddish vaudeville entertainers who performed in the nearby Hartford Opera House.

As was the tradition in many immigrant families, the children began working with their parents in the business at a young age. Sophie helped her mother with the cooking. She washed dishes and scrubbed floors, sometimes working late into the night. She attended the Brown School in Hartford, but after a long night of hard work in the restaurant she often found it difficult to stay awake in class. One class kept her awake, however—the music class where she learned to sing the popular songs of the day. She discovered she had the strongest voice of any girl in the school and soon began singing in the restaurant, entertaining the customers as they ate. She learned by heart the songs the local performers sang in the nearby theaters and sang their own songs back to them when they came in to dinner, exhibiting all the emotion she could muster.

Sophie was a heavy young girl, but the performers enjoyed being entertained by the chubby girl with the blond hair and often tipped her for her efforts. Most tips would go to her mother to help with the family finances, but sometimes the tips paid for Sophie and her friend Dora to attend Saturday matinees at Poli's Vaudeville Theater or the Hartford Opera House. Sophie, Dora, and Sophie's sister Anna began entering amateur contests in the local park, where Sophie sang and accompanied the other girls on the piano. Soon audiences asked for her, calling "Give us the fat girl." It was then that Sophie began to suspect that if she could sing and make people laugh, being overweight might not matter. She began to dream of a career in show business.

She was still dreaming of that career in show business when she graduated from high school, but she was also desperate for any means of escape from the drudgery of the restaurant kitchen. That escape came in the form of Louis Tuck, a young man from the neighborhood who, after a few dates, convinced Sophie to marry him in 1900. "We'll have lots of fun," he promised, and the young couple eloped to nearby Holyoke, Massachusetts. When Sophie's parents were told the news, they were shocked and insisted on a "proper Orthodox wedding" before the couple lived together. Soon after, Sophie became pregnant, and the young couple moved in with her parents to save money.

Sophie soon discovered that life with Louis Tuck was anything but fun. She found herself back working in her parents' restaurant, living in their home. She issued Louis an ultimatum: either make more money so they could have their own home or she would leave. But it was Louis who packed a suitcase and left. Sophie became desperate, fearful that she would never realize her own dream of a life in show business. She told her mother she was taking a two-week vacation, boarded the train bound for New York City, and watched the face of her baby son Albert recede in the distance. She knew she would not come back. She told herself it was the only way to carve a better life for herself, for her parents, and her son. As she remembered in her autobiography, *Some of These Days*, she told herself, "I had to say over and over 'it's only by getting out, making something of yourself, making real money, that you can do the most for Son and for Mama who has done so much for you.' " Sophie Tuck, changed to Tucker, was on her way.

The following months were difficult ones for Sophie as she trudged through the streets of New York looking for work as a singer. She had brought one hundred dollars with her from home, which she kept in a small bag hanging on her waist, and as the weeks went by she felt the bag become lighter and lighter as she paid for food and rent. She finally found work singing in a string of small restaurants, nightclubs, and cafés, singing hundreds of songs a night, sometimes just for her supper. After a successful appearance at the Chris Brown Amateur Night, she convinced agent Joe Woods to promote her, but there was a catch. Joe Woods thought her excess weight made her so unattractive that the audience would only listen to her if she wore blackface makeup. He began billing her as a "World Renowned Coon Shouter" and booked her in a string of theaters for twenty-five dollars a week.

It is difficult today to understand the historic popularity of the blackface performer, a practice that present-day audiences would consider racially insulting. But from the years following the Civil War until the early days of the twentieth century it was an entertainment form popular with both white and black performers. White performers usually wore blackface to sing "minstrel" type music, songs and skits supposedly reminiscent of the bumbling antics of the Negro slave, or "coon." Blackface performers who sang southern songs were called "coon shouters." Black performers sometimes performed in blackface to ridicule the white performers who were ridiculing them. Many respected actors and singers, such as Al Jolson, Eddie Cantor, and Judy Garland, performed regularly in blackface, and it was generally believed that they were not racists but simply following the customs of the day.

Sophie appeared in blackface for a very different reason—her booking agent insisted she was "too big and ugly" for any audience to accept her as a white performer. When her show was booked in Meriden, Connecticut, not too far from Hartford, she did not tell her family she was performing nearby for fear they would come to see her. "I couldn't bear to have them know I went on in blackface," she later said. It was only after her suitcase was lost in Boston and she was forced to go on without the blackface makeup that she was finally able to give up the practice she had always hated.

While she traveled as a young woman alone on the vaudeville circuit, Sophie learned the business side of show business. She learned to carry her own suitcases, to purchase her own railway tickets, and to find her way by herself from city to city on the train. She learned to court publicity men in the theaters where she performed and make friends with reporters from local newspapers. Sophie always appreciated good publicity and was not above embellishing a story for effect. She began the practice of cutting out the published notices of her performances from the newspapers and pasting them in a scrapbook; she maintained a collection of those scrapbooks for her entire life.

Sophie always remembered the stagehands in the theaters and tipped them generously. "When I came back to play those houses again I had good friends that were ready to help me put my act across," she explained. And if she was lonely, as she often was, she told herself it was the cost of getting ahead, of "making good." She tried not to indulge in self-pity but always reminded herself that she was working to make a better life for her family. She saved her money and regularly sent checks home to her mother for the support of her son, and later to help her brother Moe with his college tuition.

After her triumph at the Howard Atheneum Theater in Boston—where she finally gave up the blackface—Sophie's career with the 1909 Ziegfeld Follies was short. Her first performance brought the house down, but while the audience loved her, the star of the show, Nora Bayes, resented Sophie's success and asked Mr. Ziegfeld to limit her songs. Sophie left the Follies after only four weeks. The stress of unemployment caused her to lose her voice, and what little money she had saved began to trickle away.

But Sophie Tucker was never down for long. Her voice returned, and at a benefit performance on Long Island she was spotted by agent William Morris, who offered her a job at his theater, the American Music Hall in New York City. Her salary rose from forty dollars the first week to one hundred dollars the third. Sophie began to wear more elaborate gowns and bright jewelry, and to sing songs that had a risqué, "double entendre" edge to them, such songs as "Nobody Loves a Fat Girl, but Oh, How a Fat Girl

Can Love," and "I Don't Want to Be Thin." Sophie never apologized for her weight, but instead sought to elicit the audience's sympathy for her as a heavy girl who nevertheless dressed well and worked hard to entertain them. Although critics sometimes made fun of her size—a critic once began his piece with "speaking of elephants and Sophie Tucker"—audiences loved her.

She made the rounds of songwriters' offices, always looking for new songs to keep her act fresh and new, abiding by the advice she always gave to other performers: "Get something new. Keep fresh. Don't get stale, singing the same songs over and over." Finally, in 1910, Sophie realized one of her dreams—she saw her name up in lights over the Criterion Theatre in Atlantic City, New Jersey. She ran out with a camera and took a picture of it. Sophie Tucker had finally arrived at the "big time."

Whenever Sophie played New York City, she would send train fare for her mother, sister Anna, and son Albert, to come down and visit. Son, as Albert was called, was growing up. Sophie sent her parents money to buy a house and to send Son to a good boarding school. But Sophie had very few mothering skills and never established a close relationship with her son, who thought of her sister Anna as his mother.

By 1911 Sophie was making $500 a week on the vaudeville circuit. She began to experiment with theater, taking parts in several plays and singing at private parties later in the evenings. One day, on the advice of her black maid Mollie, she listened to a song, "Some of These Days," written by a young black composer, Shelton Brooks. As she described it in her 1945 autobiography by the same name, "The minute I heard 'Some of these Days' I could have kicked myself for almost losing it. A song like that . . . had everything. Hasn't it proved it? I've been singing it for thirty years, made it my theme song . . . and always audiences have loved it and asked for it. Later Shelton Brooks wrote 'Darktown Strutters Ball' but nothing else he ever did touched 'Some of These Days.' "

In 1913 Sophie achieved what she considered the high point in her career, when she returned home triumphantly to Hartford to headline at the Poli Theatre. She remembered only too well visiting the theater as a young girl, hanging around the stage door, asking the performers to come and eat at her parents' restaurant. Now her name was on billboards all over town announcing, "Sophie Tucker, The Pride of Hartford." Her parents welcomed her to the house she had helped them buy, her son was home from school, and, of course, her show was a hit. Sophie said later that her appearance in Hartford in 1913 was "the most wonderful week of my life." One critic reported that the crowds didn't applaud because she was local but because "she is an accomplished, talented girl, without equal in vaudeville as a singer of ragtime songs."

In August 1914, as the country was preparing to enter World War I, Sophie scored another personal triumph when she played at the Palace Theater in New York City. The Palace was vaudeville's most prestigious theater. To play there was the dream of all performers, "something to boast about for the rest of your life." Sophie performed there with a young piano player, Frank Westphal, and the duo was acclaimed in local papers as a huge success.

In 1914 Louis Tuck, Sophie's estranged husband, unexpectedly died, and soon after Sophie married Frank Westphal. As World War I progressed, she began a practice she continued for the rest of her life of performing for charity, raising and donating funds to deserving causes. Throughout World War I she raised over four million dollars to send tobacco products to U.S. troops in Europe and was hailed as "The Smoke Angel of Our Boys." She contributed heavily to Jewish charities, especially the Jewish War Relief Campaign. Sophie always maintained her Jewish faith, fasting on High Holy days, but ironically she violated one of the main tenets of the religion by continuing to work on those days.

By 1920 Sophie Tucker was an undisputed show business star. She appeared in the Sophie Tucker Room at Reisenweber's Restaurant at 58th Street and 8th Avenue in New York, introducing such sentimental ballads as "M-O-T-H-E-R—A Name that Means the World to Me."

In 1922 she convinced William Morris to book her on tour in England and crossed the Atlantic for the first time since her arrival in America as an infant. Nervous about appearing before what she feared were staid English audiences, she took pains to research British colloquialisms and assess British tastes by attending other shows herself. Sophie soon discovered the English audiences were more tolerant of her risqué, double entendre songs that eventually earned her the nickname of "The Last of the Red Hot Mamas," but would not tolerate any jokes about the Royal Family. The British audiences loved her. One critic described her as "a big, fat blond genius with a dynamic personality and amazing vitality." Sophie brought a new young pianist, Ted Shapiro, to England to accompany her because she was concerned that a British pianist "might not be up on American Jazz rhythms." Apparently the relationship was as successful as Sophie's English tour—Ted Shapiro worked for her for forty-five years.

Sophie also enjoyed a long-term, mutually profitable relationship with songwriter Jack Yellin, who wrote songs exclusively for her. Many of the songs he wrote for her were never published so no one else could sing them. But Sophie often shared songs with young singers, an unusual practice in the competitive world of show business. Successful singers usually jealously guarded their songs, but Sophie enjoyed a reputation of being more generous with her music than others.

Upon her return from her triumphant English engagement she continued to work in vaudeville theaters, restaurants, and nightclubs both in the United States and abroad. Always open to new experiences, she agreed to make a "talking" film in 1929 for Warner Brothers, *Honky Tonk*, which was not successful. But in 1932 her career began to change. Vaudeville houses closed as movie theaters attracted bigger and bigger audiences. Sophie had shared the view of many in show business who doubted the talking film industry would be successful. She later discovered how wrong she had been. "I didn't tumble to the fact," she later admitted, "that I was witnessing the birth of an era that was to bring about the death of vaudeville . . . the first bomb of the blitz that would black out the small-time and big-times houses everywhere."

Sophie tried to adapt her act to the new entertainment media, making eight films between 1929 and 1945, and appearing on radio and television variety shows when those new mediums appeared. But Sophie felt radio and television didn't do her act justice. She complained that her language was censored on air—she could not even say "hell" or "damn." She felt television gave "too much away for too little." She was always the most at ease performing before a live audience where she could work one-on-one with the audience and impose her own personal magnetism through her distinctive stage personality. She was equally comfortable performing a rousing, risqué jazz tune, such as "Who Paid the Rent for Mrs. Rip Van Winkle (When Rip Van Winkle was Away?)," or a sentimental ballad, such as "My Yiddishe Mama," one of her most popular numbers.

In 1938 Sophie was elected president of the American Federation of Actors (AFA), the first woman to hold that office. She hoped that leading the union would enable her to speak out for the rights of vaudeville and musical comedy performers at a time when other media were making inroads into the popularity of those fields. She also favored bringing the stagehands into the union with the actors. But there were ugly rumors that the leadership of the union had misappropriated funds. Sophie found herself in the center of a bitter controversy involving such show business friends as Eddie Cantor and a young Katharine Hepburn. In the end, the AFA merged with Equity's American Guild of Variety Artists.

Sophie continued to raise funds for many different charities, including Save the Children of England, Catholic Charities, Episcopal and Jewish Theatrical Guilds, and the Home for the Aged in Hartford, Connecticut, all of whom benefited from the sales of her autobiography, *Some of These Days*, published in 1945. She continued to visit England and enjoy the devotion of English fans and considered England her second home.

Throughout her career of almost sixty years, Sophie Tucker was a controversial and contradictory personality. Although she revered traditional values of home and family, she rejected the role of dependent spouse and left husband and son behind to pursue a career. Her marriage to Frank Westphal ended in 1920, and a third marriage to a former fan, Al Lackey, ended in 1928, failures Sophie attributed to the fact that she was the primary breadwinner of the family. "The greatest obstacle to my happiness as a woman is my success as an entertainer," she stated in her autobiography. Yet, she never stopped looking for the "right man."

She considered her relationship with her son and his wife to be her greatest failure, a dilemma she never resolved. Curiously, after giving him a Miami hotel, she headlined for a competitor. She loved hobnobbing with the royal and famous but at the same time felt a real affinity for members of the working-class, especially stagehands, bus drivers, and chorus girls. Although she sang earthy, ribald musical numbers, she dressed in exquisite, elegant, sequined gowns, often complemented by elaborate, feathered headdresses. She barely finished high school, yet in 1955 she endowed a chair in Theater Arts at Brandeis University. She embodied the quintessential immigrant success story of hard work and generosity toward others. She worked for her entire life until her death from lung cancer on February 10, 1966, in New York City.

Her introduction in 1928 as "The Last of the Red Hot Mamas" seemed appropriately prophetic. When Sophie Tucker died in 1966, she was one of the few entertainers to have ever sustained the heat of such undisputed, controversial but enduring stardom.

MARGARET FOGARTY RUDKIN

1897–1967

Founder of Pepperidge Farm

*I*t was 1937 and the young woman, clutching her curious set of parcels, hurried from the train in Grand Central Station in New York City. She crossed the street with an air of determination and headed for the food specialty shop of Charles and Company. When she reached the shop she hesitated, at once gripped with fear. Suddenly she realized how bizarre it might seem to the store manager to have a young woman ask for an interview, armed with a loaf of homemade bread, a quarter-pound of butter, and a knife. Perhaps she should turn around, head back to her comfortable Connecticut farm, and write a letter to the manager of the shop instead.

But she had come this far, she decided, and would not turn back. She entered the respectable old establishment and asked for the manager, who eyed with skepticism her loaf of bread and especially her knife. But when she offered him a sample of the bread, topped with a generous slather of the butter, his mood began to change. "My goodness," he said, "that's just the kind of bread my mother made when I was a boy." Without hesitation he ordered twenty-four loaves to be delivered the next day.

Margaret Fogarty Rudkin

Margaret (Peg) Rudkin was ecstatic. Here was just the break she was looking for: a successful, well-known retailer who would distribute her bread to both her mail-order customers and his own customers as well. She boarded her train and returned to Connecticut delighted with her newfound good fortune.

But when she got home reality struck. How would she get twenty-four loaves of freshly baked bread back to New York City by the next morning? Then she remembered—her husband took the commuter train to New York City every morning. Surely he wouldn't mind delivering a package for her on his way to work. The next morning she packed up the loaves of bread, and to stave off any objections her husband might have, she waited until he was ready to leave to thrust the package into his hand. "If he had stopped to argue," she explained later, "he would have missed the train, so off he went with the package."

Henry Rudkin took the package of freshly baked bread on the train that day—and packages every day after that—and delivered it to Charles and Company. He soon found an obliging Red Cap who would deliver it across the street for him for the grand sum of twenty-five cents. Soon he was taking two packages on the train, then three. Finally, the demand for his wife's homemade bread became so great that they had to turn the delivery job over to Railway Express Company. The baking company called Pepperidge Farm was on its way.

No one could have been more surprised by the success of the Pepperidge Farm than Peg Rudkin herself. She once admitted that when she began the company in 1937 at the age of forty she had "never made a loaf of bread in my life." Yet, she began a company that in the space of just a few years became one of the most successful and well-known food purveyors in the world, with customers in every state and in many foreign countries, eventually becoming a household name that almost every English-speaking person recognizes.

Peg Fogarty was born in New York City on September 14, 1897, the eldest of five children of Joseph Fogarty and Margaret Healey. The family lived with Peg's grandparents in the Tudor City area of Manhattan, where her childhood passed serenely in a world of cobblestone streets and tall, narrow brownstone houses with wide, welcoming front steps. Those front steps were a favorite gathering place for the children, where in the dusk of early evening they would sit and watch for the lamplighter to come by and light the street lamps with a long, flaming taper.

Peg's grandmother was the household cook. She had been born in Ireland and carried her family recipes with her from her homeland, most of them written only in her memory. Like many cooks that lived in another era, Peg's grandmother and mother wrote very few recipes down on paper. When Peg started cooking she once said the recipes simply came "out of her head" and took life from the memories of her childhood.

Meals in the Fogarty household were usually simple fare, with no "fancy stuff and sauces." There were hearty soups and stews and fresh foods that reflected the season—strawberries in June, sweet cold watermelon in the summer, crisp grapes in the fall, hearty rice puddings and custards in the winter. Although Peg claimed in adulthood that she had never baked a loaf of bread until 1937, as a child she learned to cook many other dishes and by the age of ten was proficient at the preparation of such staples as baking powder biscuits and chocolate layer cake. "Fast foods" or any kind of pre-pared foods were still in the future. Everything was made "from scratch," with basic, wholesome ingredients. Her family also canned fruits and vegetables throughout the summer, enough to last them through the long, cold New York winters.

When Peg was twelve years old her grandmother died, and the family moved to Flushing, Queens, a suburb of New York City. She attended public schools, studied mathematics and finance, and graduated from high school as valedictorian of her class. After graduation she accepted a job in a bank and later worked in a brokerage firm where she met a young man named Henry Rudkin. The couple were married in 1923, and in 1926 they purchased 125 acres in Fairfield, Connecticut, where they built a house and farm buildings, and where both were determined to live "a real country life."

In her *Pepperidge Farm Cookbook*, published in 1963, Peg describes that life in nostalgic, loving detail. The couple discovered that a large number of a variety of sourgum trees, also called pepperidge trees, grew on the property and decided to call their new home Pepperidge Farm. They sent for pamphlets and publications from the Department of Agriculture and, following the department's directions, they planted more than 500 apple trees on the property, along with pear, plum, and peach trees. They grew vegetables, raised chickens and turkeys, even experimented with raising pigs and beef, which they fattened with homegrown field corn. They churned butter, cured hams and bacon, and froze their own beef. Peg canned jams and jellies and developed recipes for homemade mincemeat and sauerkraut. Three sons were born to the couple, and in addition to developing the farm, Henry enjoyed golfing, hunting, and polo. Life was serene; it seemed they had achieved the wonderful "country life" they had dreamed of.

But that life changed drastically in 1932 when Henry suffered a polo accident and was unable to work, confined to the farm for six months. Peg dismissed most of the help, sold Henry's polo ponies and horses, and helped support the family by selling apples from the estate's orchard and turkeys from their poultry farm. But her business ventures turned serious in 1937 when she baked, out of concern for her son's health, her first loaf of bread—the loaf of bread that started a financial empire.

When Peg's youngest son, Mark, was nine years old he suffered from asthma and various food allergies. His doctor was concerned that food additives used in commercial baking and cooking might be causing his problems. He recommended a basic diet of only natural foods—fresh fruits and vegetables, natural sugars such as molasses and honey, and stone-ground, whole wheat flour, a type of flour that contains wheat germ and is rich in vitamin B_1. Peg had learned the benefits of fresh, natural foods from her grandmother as a child, but she had never baked bread and was unfamiliar with stone-ground whole wheat.

She purchased whole wheat flour from a New England gristmill and began experimenting with it, developing her own recipes for pancakes and muffins, using no white flour or white sugar. When those proved successful she "got out all the cookbooks I owned, read all the directions and started in" on her first loaf of bread. "That first loaf should have been sent to the Smithsonian Institution as a sample of bread from the Stone Age," she commented in her cookbook, "for it was hard as a rock and about one inch high." Peg had never used yeast before and was unfamiliar with balancing the temperature controls necessary for its success. But after a few more trials and a generous application of butter, honey, and molasses, she achieved success, baking a bread that her family found delicious. The true test of the bread for her was when her children ate it without being told to "eat it because it's good for you."

Peg told her son's doctor about the bread and how she made it using only whole wheat flour. After tasting a sample he ordered some for himself and his patients. Several other doctors heard of the bread and wanted it for their patients. As word of the delicious and nutritious homemade bread became known throughout the community, orders began to pour in and, with the help of one employee, Peg began a small mail-order business, baking the bread, wrapping it, and mailing it to a growing list of customers. The enterprise soon outgrew the farm kitchen and was moved first to a converted garage on the property and then into a larger building that had once stabled Henry's polo ponies.

Peg approached her local grocer and offered him the bread to sell in his shop. Regular commercial bread was then selling for ten cents a loaf, but she charged the grocer twenty cents and suggested he sell it for twenty-five cents. Although dubious, the grocer agreed, and soon other grocers were asking for the bread, all clamoring to sell the homemade product, even at the unheard-of price. Her successful trip to Charles and Company in New York City effectively expanded the company's territory. She then began making a white bread that eventually became one of her company's most popular items.

From the beginning the key to Pepperidge Farm's success was the ingredients Peg insisted on using—only wholesome, natural products—and the methods by which they were processed. The whole wheat flour was stone-ground, using the old-fashioned method of grinding the wheat between two large stones, the upper stone (sometimes called the "runner" stone) and the lower stone (sometimes called the "bed" or "nether" stone). The lower stone stays still while the upper stone revolves. The stones never touch. Both stones have sharp surface furrows to provide more efficient grinding of the grain and to promote the passage of air between them so the flour is forced out to a bin underneath. The flour must be kept cool during the process; thus the stones must revolve at just the right speed to prevent overheating.

Wheat flour contains all the wheat, including the germ, which is rich in nutrients, and it also contains more gluten, which makes the dough elastic and allows for expansion during baking. When Peg made white bread she used only unbleached flour, avoiding white flour that was bleached with chemicals. She also used only grade A butter and the highest quality honey, molasses, and fresh milk.

As Pepperidge Farm became more successful and its need for

more stone-ground flour grew, the Rudkins had four gristmills restored throughout the New England area, purchased their own wheat, and kept a close watch on the process in those mills, making sure they adhered to the farm's high standards. Eventually the company began grinding its own wheat into flour, which finally offered it total control over the end product. By the end of 1938 the company was baking 4,000 loaves of bread each week.

In 1939 Pepperidge Farm received a boost of favorable publicity in various newspapers and magazines, by far the most influential being an article entitled "Bread, de Luxe," published in the *Reader's Digest* and written by J. D. Ratcliff. The article engendered much favorable attention and yielded orders for the bread from all over the United States and even from some foreign countries.

By 1940 the business had grown so much that the Rudkins decided to move it to facilities in nearby Norwalk, where they rented an empty service station while planning the modern bakery they would build. But World War II effectively put those plans on hold. Pepperidge Farm had difficulties finding goods during the war but was able to struggle along because it had always provided much of its own product, including home-churned butter. The new facilities, although small, allowed the company to add new products to its line, including melba toast and pound cake. After the war, Pepperidge Farm was finally able to build a modern bakery in Norwalk.

Although the company had been started by Peg, it was always a family affair and included the labor of both Henry and their three sons. In 1949 Henry resigned his partnership in the firm of McClure, Jones and Company, where he had worked for years, to devote most of his time to Pepperidge Farm. Henry handled the general finances, managed sales, and purchased supplies and equipment. Peg concentrated on dealing with the personnel and on the products themselves, always experimenting with new ideas and recipes. Even when Pepperidge Farm expanded and built two plants in Pennsylvania to serve the markets there, the company still adhered to the original recipes, and Peg still insisted that the dough be made in small batches and each loaf kneaded by hand. It was only with great reluctance that they agreed to install commercial machines to cut and wrap the bread; Peg always maintained that old-fashioned bread should only be cut when eaten.

In 1950 Peg began appearing as "Maggie Rudkin" in television advertisements for Pepperidge Farm, and the company continued to grow. By 1953 it was producing 77,000 loaves of bread each week. It continued to add to its product line, securing frozen pastry from a company in New Hampshire, and in 1956 it secured the recipes for luxury cookies from the Delacre Company, a respected bakery in Belgium.

Since Pepperidge Farm products contained no preservatives and since company policy decreed that they should be left on store shelves for only two days, many loaves were returned to the plant each day. Peg dealt with these returns by turning them into herb-flavored stuffing, a product that became one of the company's best-selling items. Throughout the 1950s Pepperidge Farm's product line grew to include more than fifty items.

In 1957, to celebrate the twentieth anniversary of the founding of Pepperidge Farm, each of the firm's employees—mostly women—contributed one dollar to purchase a gift for Peg: a copy of a rare cookbook, a fifteenth-century classic, *De Honesta Voluptate et Valetudine*, by Bartholomaeus de Platina. Written in medieval Latin and printed in Venice in 1475, the book became a treasured addition to her collection of historic cookbooks. Even more touching than the gift was the scroll that was presented with the book—a scroll that every single one of the 1,000 employees had signed. Entire families worked for the company for years and were devoted to its founders, who both respected them and paid them generously.

By 1960 Pepperidge Farm was the largest independent bakery in the United States, with sales in excess of $32 million, and more than 1,000 employees. Despite their phenomenal success, Peg and her husband decided to relinquish family ownership of the firm, and in 1960 they sold Pepperidge Farm to the Campbell Soup Company for Campbell stock worth about $28 million. Pepperidge Farm remained an autonomous company within Campbell Soup, Peg became a director of Campbell Soup while continuing her presidency of Pepperidge Farm, and Henry maintained the seat of chairman of the board of Pepperidge Farm. The Rudkins were finally able to spend some time relaxing on an estate in County Carlow, Ireland, that they had purchased in 1953.

In 1962 the Rudkins' son William became president of Pepperidge Farm, Henry retired, and Peg assumed the position of chairman of the board. Henry Rudkin died in 1966, and Peg Fogarty Rudkin died of breast cancer on June 1, 1967. She was sixty-nine years old.

In her youth Peg was described as "slim and sophisticated, with gorgeous red hair, green eyes and a milk-white complexion." She was raised in a time when women were expected to follow the traditional feminine paths of early marriage and motherhood and not to bother themselves with the intricacies of the business world.

But life dictated otherwise. When her husband became ill, she drew upon her own personal resources to help support her family. When her son became ill with allergies and asthma, she searched for a natural way to help him regain his health and in the process stumbled upon a business that would become an empire.

Today Pepperidge Farm remains a growing, thriving business, with annual sales estimated at more than a billion dollars, and over 200 million loaves of bread sold each year. Its product line still includes the very same items that Peg began making in her home in 1937—the ever-popular whole wheat and white bread—as well as products later added to the line: rolls, cookies, stuffing, puff pastry, and the best loved snack of all, Goldfish, which celebrated its fortieth anniversary in 2002. Pepperidge Farm remains a living testament to the beliefs and efforts of both Peg and Henry Rudkin and their sons. Their success developed both from a belief in natural healthy foods and from an abiding respect for such virtues as hard work, diligence, and a devotion to excellence that dictated they use only the best ingredients in their products. Those ideals carried them through the early years of the development of the company, as well as the prosperous years when the company grew beyond either Peg's or Henry's wildest dreams.

And it all began with a loaf of bread—hard as a rock—that turned to pure gold.

EVA LUTZ
BUTLER

1897–1969

Teacher, Historian,
Anthropologist

 $\mathcal{T}$ he building stands square and strong, built of bricks forged in another time. The massive iron-faced doors are fastened with solid bolts that clang impressively when the doors are swung open. The structure clings to the edge of a very busy country lane, where it exudes both character and strength, qualities demanded by society for the shelter of its most valuable materials. When it was built in 1856 and for many years after, those materials were the cash and securities of its neighbors whose treasures were tucked safely inside its vault.

Today the building is home to treasures of a very different kind—treasures that, unlike cash and securities, are irreplaceable. The Mystic National Bank building is now home to The Indian & Colonial Research Center, which houses the collection of Eva Lutz Butler, local archeologist, historian, anthropologist, writer, and general expert on the history of the Groton, Connecticut area, including that of its Native Americans. The list of her occupations is lengthy—the list of her talents even lengthier, and the scope of her rich collection bears perfect witness to both.

But although her collection is housed in a former treasure chest of sorts, Eva Lutz Butler was no miser—indeed just the opposite. She worked tirelessly for more than forty years, amassing a collection of books, papers, photographs, artifacts, and diaries that carefully

THE BUTLER FAMILY (WWW.CROMWELLBUTLERS.COM)

Eva Lutz Butler on her wedding day

document the history of her corner of the globe and its inhabitants for the express purpose of both sharing it with present-day citizens and preserving it for the use of future generations.

Eva Lutz was born on November 13, 1897, in Pleasantville, New Jersey, eldest of the three children of William Lutz and Laura Breish. Both parents had been born in Pennsylvania; her father made his living as a house painter and carpenter. As a young girl Eva loved the outdoors and enjoyed ice skating in winter, hiking and nature study in the summer. Her childhood was spent in Pleasantville, attending the public schools, vacationing with relatives in Pennsylvania, and helping to raise her two younger siblings, Catherine and Frank.

In September 1916, when Eva was in her senior year, Pleasantville High School welcomed a new teacher to its staff, a young Yale graduate by the name of Sylvester Benjamin Butler. Sylvester had been born in Cromwell, Connecticut, and after a brief stint in business he came to Pleasantville to teach history and algebra at the high school. Sylvester was a serious young man, devoted to his family, and given to writing long newsy letters home to his mother every Sunday evening. It is through those letters that we learn of his life in Pleasantville and his growing affection for Eva.

Sylvester tells of his friendship with a fellow teacher, Miss Tolbert, who is an "ardent suffragist," a position that does not seem to offend him. Miss Tolbert has taken under her wing a young student named Eva Lutz. Slowly, over the last waning months of 1916, mention of Eva begins to filter into his letters home. He describes in detail the activities that all three share: festive lunches, long walks through the countryside, picnics, and skating parties. Eventually his mother must have noticed and commented on the waning of information about Miss Tolbert and the corresponding waxing of details about Eva Lutz, for in a letter dated February 4, 1917, Sylvester explains, "Eva Lutz, whom I have spoken of quite frequently, and whom you asked about, is a sort of protégé of Miss Tolbert's, at least I suppose one would call her so. They spend a great deal of time together and are very congenial in their tastes, and beside that, Miss Tolbert is very much interested in the girl and her future. The young lady has an attractive personality, she is a girl with a good mind, an original thinker, and a lady to the core, she takes a wholesome enjoyment in outdoor life of all kinds, and has, I think, a great deal of promise." Eva must have thought he, too, "had a great deal of promise." When Sylvester joined the Army in May 1917, they wrote each other every day, touching, revealing letters that chronicled a tender courtship.

Sylvester's letters were formal, filled with myriad details about his daily life. In contrast, Eva's were chatty, giving evidence of a cheerful disposition coupled with seemingly boundless energy. She worked as a stenographer during the day and spent her free time gardening, reading, gathering flowers, canning fruits, and writing to Sylvester. When they became engaged in April 1918, the signature lines on their letters tellingly changed from "Your friend as always" to "Dearest," and "Forever yours." After a tour of duty in France during World War I, Sylvester returned home and they were married on August 4, 1919. Their first and only child, a son named Sewall, was born a year later in August 1920.

Over the next few years the family traveled as Sylvester held several positions. From 1926 until 1928 he studied for a graduate degree at Columbia University in New York City, and Eva passed her time writing educational materials on the Manhattan Indians for the Industrial Arts Cooperative. It was her first experience with the study of Native American history, and she was intrigued. In 1931 Sylvester became Superintendent of the Groton School District, and Eva's life as an archeologist and historian finally began in earnest.

Eva's own words tell the story best, as she wrote in a biographical sketch:

> When Mr. Butler went to Groton as Superintendent of Schools we were in the heart of the Pequot country and I was thrilled with the opportunity to find out about Indians. I knew something about Indians—almost all the wrong things. I had just gotten over the belief that they all lived in beautiful painted teepees, rode about in birch bark canoes, wore feathered headdresses, etc. and believed that now I would see for myself.
>
> There were very few Indians left in Connecticut, I soon found out. Most of them lived the way we did. A few were proud of being Indians, but many were ashamed of the fact that they had Indian ancestry.

Eva was intrigued and a bit saddened by the fact that so many of the Indians took so little pride in their heritage. She set about to discover their history for herself. She began by researching court probate records, land records, and diaries. She researched where the Indians had lived, who had owned what parcels of land, where they had traveled, and with whom they had traded. Most of the documents were inscribed on yellowed, fraying papers, in illegible scrawls almost impossible to decipher. Eva spent hours copying the papers longhand, typing them later, and filing them in loose-leaf notebooks.

She pored over such collections as the Pynchon Papers, housed in the Smith College Library in Northhampton, Massachusetts, and in the library at Springfield, Massachusetts. William Pynchon was the founder of Springfield in the spring of 1636, a town which was once part of Connecticut. The settlement was founded, in large part, to take advantage of fur-trading opportunities along the Connecticut

River. The Pynchon Papers offer the Indian names for the thirteen months of the Indian year, as well as the Indian names for many of the local animals.

The account books of traders John and Samuel Chandler, housed in the Connecticut State Library in Hartford, detail their business activities with the Indians, including their trades with the nearby Nehantic Indians. Whatever Eva could not find in Connecticut archives she searched for in the archives of the surrounding states of New York, Rhode Island, and Massachusetts.

In 1936 Eva decided to travel to the Southwest to catch a glimpse of a real living Native American culture, and to experience firsthand an archeological dig. She wrote from Sante Fe, New Mexico, that she had visited Native American cliff dwellings hollowed out of rock, believing herself to be one of the first white women to do so. She purchased original pottery from the natives and witnessed their native dances, including the Snake dance and the Eagle dance. Her research on the lives of the Southwest Indians helped to illuminate the lives of the Indians nearer her home. She returned home at the end of the summer "filled with ideas and a little sobered, too." Eva wrote to a friend:

> Determined to see Indians for myself I went to the Southwest on a dig with the University of New Mexico. It was thrilling—learning to dig in the ground for history, to dig carefully with a trowel, whisk brooms and tooth brushes . . . with records being kept of where, how and under what conditions everything was found, it was fabulous training. . . . Many people in the Southwest and one or two teachers believed that we in the East thought the world began in 1620 when the Pilgrims landed, that we had killed off all our Indians, dug up all our archeology and put

gas stations on top of everything. It was a sobering thought, and I set out to disprove it.

She continued researching and copying records, carefully reconstructing a history of the Indians of which even they themselves were ignorant. She struck up friendships with members of the local tribes that were still in the area, Martha Ann Langevin, a member of the Mashantucket Pequots, and Gladys Tantaquidgeon of the Mohegan tribe. She persuaded them to let her photograph them.

In addition to her research on the local Indians, Eva took particular interest in the lives of ordinary colonial women, and delighted in reading and recording entries from their journals and diaries. Through these fragile records the women's voices still resonate, relating not only tales of hard work and perilous childbirth, but sometimes stories of ill-fated love affairs and adulterous relationships that usually brought only the woman public censure. Through such detailed research Eva cast a fascinating twentieth century light on the societal inequities and political frailties suffered by women throughout history.

In 1939 Eva fell in love with the James Woodbridge house, which had been built in 1732, on Gallup Road in Ledyard, Connecticut. She could have bought the house, barns, and acreage for about $1,900 but was dissuaded from doing so by Sylvester, who was perhaps wary of buying such an old house. The Butler's son, Sewall, was enrolled as a freshman at the University of New Mexico, and Eva decided to join him there, enrolling in the University herself to continue her studies of archeology and Native American history. Returning home in 1941 with a Bachelor of Arts Degree, she finally bought the old James Woodbridge house (although the price had risen to $2,800) and began filling it up with her writings, books, manuscripts, and copies of documents—filling a historic house with the raiment of history.

Primary sources were sacred to Eva. She scorned secondary versions of historic events, and her arguments with many secondary sources are still evidenced by her indignant notes scribbled in the margins of manuscripts. As the collection grew she sought out rare books, but with a limited budget she often had to content herself with copying those books she could not afford to buy:

> I was unable to afford the rare books then that I wanted and needed, so I set out to type whole books of information on the Northeast—*Mourt's Relation* . . . Roger Williams's *Key to the Language,* William Wood's *New England Prospect.* Thomas Morton's *New English Canann*—ever so many others. I filled notebook after notebook with excerpts from original sources, putting articles under source headings, collecting, sorting, cataloguing, until I had over two thousand notebooks and a book of indices.
>
> I was like the ant gathering grains of sand or the sparrow gathering grains of wheat one at a time from the granary. I'd get a notebook and another notebook and another notebook until I'd filled up one room then another room then another room, until six rooms of our house were burdened with my notes of the past.

In 1946 Eva was awarded a master's degree from the University of Pennsylvania, and she began teaching extension courses in her home to students at Willimantic State College, now Eastern Connecticut State University. Using archeology as a teaching tool, she led students in digs in West Mystic, at Millstone in Waterford, Connecticut, and at sites throughout Ledyard, where they often unearthed projectile points (more commonly known as arrowheads), and pottery shards and sometimes even bits of skeletons.

(It was rumored that she kept a portion of a skeleton she had unearthed in a long chest in her home.) She taught college courses in American Folklore, Spring Nature Study, and Colonial History, which must have been her favorite, since she considered any history after the Revolution to be "too modern."

One former student remembered that Eva's enthusiasm for teaching history was not even dimmed one summer by a broken leg. The students, hearing of her injury, were sympathetic but happily assumed their courses would be so much easier—a summer spent "sitting under the shade trees of the Butler Estate on Gallup Hill" with Eva limited to simply lecturing. But according to the astonished student "it never happened": "Believe it or not we never missed one planned nature walk as prescribed by the course. . . . Over hill and dale and stone walls Eva Butler led her team, observing and collecting specimens of wild flowers, leaves, moss, ferns, and 'life' in the local pond. Her leg cast never slowed her down or hindered her for one minute. In fact, she often reached home base before many of us, showing less fatigue, and ready to go on with the next project."

Indeed, Eva's energy still seemed boundless. She visited the state legislature and lobbied on behalf of Native Americans, leading campaigns for the preservation of Indian burial grounds and home sites. In 1958 Eva finally found a home for many of the Indian relics she had been collecting and opened the Tomaquag Indian Museum in Ashaway, Rhode Island, where the local Indians' way of life could be reconstructed. School children were invited to visit the museum, to see how the Indians lived and to join in the celebration of Indian ceremonies. They took part in the "sugaring off" process that the Indians used to tap maple syrup from trees. They learned about the Indians' methods of tracking game. They listened to Indian legends and tales. Each young visitor received a copy of the deed to the surrounding Mohegan countryside, dated 1705, showing the presence not only of the homes of the settlers but of the "sneersucks," or cave dwellings, of the resident tribes.

Eva complemented her college courses with booklets that she wrote herself to illustrate tribal life—booklets with such titles as *Around the Pond* and *Beginnings of the Pequot Plantation.* The booklets illustrated with elaborate sketches how Indian children lived, the clothes they wore, how Indian babies were cared for and how young Indian children passed their time and what responsibilities they were expected to fulfill. "Indian girls were taught to make bowls and mats for the houses," she wrote. "The boys were trained to use their bows and arrows from childhood." She established a children's museum in New London that eventually became the Thames Science Center.

Despite being encouraged to do so, she never formally published any of her writings, except for one book entitled *Two Little Indians Dip Their Sheep,* published by E. M. Hale & Company in 1937. The book was a result of her 1936 trip to visit Indian tribes in New Mexico and related the story of an Indian family and their children's responsibility for the care of the family's flock of sheep. Throughout the story Eva skillfully wove evidential information about Indian life and completed the book with a glossary of Indian words. She wrote carefully researched papers about such diverse topics as the sweat houses in the southern New England area and the dogs of the northeast Woodland Indians, all of which went unpublished. She still had not learned all there was to know about the subjects, she insisted. She had found many errors in historic documents over her years of research and was loathe to perpetrate such mistakes herself. "I should have begun writing long ago, long ago," she once confessed to a friend, "but I wanted it to be so perfect."

She continued to fill up her famous notebooks, storing them at home until the floors of the old James Woodbridge house fairly sagged under their weight. After she suffered a heart attack in April 1964, her friends and family became concerned about her health, correctly assessing that her collection needed a new home. So when the historic Mystic National Bank building became available for purchase from the Town of Stonington, her friends went into action.

The group was led by retired teacher Harry W. Nelson and included, among others, Eva's good friends Mary Virginia Goodman and local teacher Carol Kimball. In December 1965 the Indian and Colonial Research Center was incorporated as a nonprofit organization and requested the voters of Stonington to sell them the historic building for one dollar. Once the building was purchased, a $2,000 grant enabled volunteers to get to work installing shelving, replacing the heating system, and painting and refurbishing the building. Finally, the thousands of notebooks, maps, books, and manuscripts were moved from the farmhouse on Gallup Road to their new home in the former Mystic National Bank building. Typical of her modest nature, Eva steadfastly refused the suggestion that the research center be named for her.

Despite ill health Eva continued researching and responding to a voluminous correspondence, answering requests for teaching aides or genealogical information or information about the old homes in the area. When she was not feeling well she worked in bed, her papers strewn about her. At times her determination and concentration bordered on the eccentric; one friend remembered that she would often become so engrossed in her research that she would forget time and meals, sometimes not even noticing when the building she was working in closed. "More than once the 'powers that be' forgot the lady in the lower level and she was locked in until rescued by the janitor," her friend recalled.

In 1966 Eva was awarded the Award of Merit by the Connecticut League of Historical Societies and was cited as "the authority for ethno-history of New England and the most gifted interpreter of the region's Indian and Colonial History." In 1967 the American Association for State and Local History recognized her "outstanding contributions to local history."

Eva Lutz Butler died on January 20, 1969. Her death elicited an outpouring of affection and respect. She was remembered for being generous to a fault, for never begrudging the time it took to help, for always trying to inspire others with her love of nature, her reverence for the Indians and their history. "Eva never refused a request for information," her friend Carol Kimball remembered. "She would answer a child's query just as carefully as she would reply to a learned professor." Eva recognized the need to preserve the history of her small part of the globe at a time when it was certainly more fashionable to destroy "our archeology and put gas stations on top of everything." She spent a good deal of her life single-mindedly pursuing the goal of preservation.

Today, through the work of dedicated volunteers, The Indian & Colonial Research Center continues Eva Butler's work of keeping the past alive. In addition to her collection of books and records, the center is home to an impressive collection of locally discovered Indian projectile points, peace pipes, pottery, examples of rare weaving, dolls, and baskets. A collection of oral history tapes adds a new dimension of historical study. There are local family coats of arms, photographs, glass plate negatives, historic maps of the surrounding area, and hundreds of rare books. And if one listens carefully, one might just hear Eva's cheerful and encouraging voice echoing softly through the research center's busy, crowded rooms: "Keep your eyes open," she might be saying, as she often did. "The study of history can often start right in your own backyard."

The Indian & Colonial Research Center is located on Main Street (Route 27) in Old Mystic, Connecticut 06372, Phone: (860) 536–9771, Web site: www.geocities.com/icrc06372/.

GLADYS TANTAQUIDGEON

1899–

Mohegan Medicine Woman

*G*ladys Tantaquidgeon remembers exactly the day in 1904 when she began her training as a medicine woman of the Mohegan tribe. She was barely five years old and had been invited by three elder women of her tribe to accompany them on one of their walks through the fields and woods. The women often made these treks to gather herbs and plants to use as medicines in their healing practices.

Gladys called the women "Nanu," or grandmother, and all three held positions of importance in her life. Her great-aunt Emma Fielding Baker was the chief medicine woman of the tribe, a position she had inherited from her grandmother. It was she who kept the written tribal records and preserved the tribal history. Lydia Fielding and Mercy Ann Nonesuch Mathews were both experts at preparing curative medicines and developing healing practices. The three were a familiar sight, roaming the forests and fields throughout the Mohegan tribal lands, gathering such plants as bloodroot, motherwort, and ginseng to treat the tribe's ills. Gladys herself had watched them depart to work in the fields and

TANTAQUIDGEON MUSEUM

Gladys Tantaquidgeon

return with their herbs many times.

But this time it would be different. This time Gladys was invited to join them, not as a tagalong granddaughter, but as a respected member of the tribe who was being groomed for an important position. The women were growing older. They had already discussed which little girl would be best suited to replace them in time, and they all agreed that small, soft-spoken Gladys showed the most promise. Though she was still very young, they could tell that she was bright enough to learn their skills and honorable enough to be entrusted with their secrets. The grandmothers took her by the hand and began to show her how to choose the best plants to be gathered, dried, and used for medicine and food.

Gladys knew that something special was happening that day. There was magic in the air—the magic of the Nanus. Children love magic and Gladys was no exception. She listened to the Nanus because she had been taught to respect her elders. She helped them choose various plants and herbs. As she grew she would follow the Nanus' teachings and learn their medicine. She would travel far to study the white man's way and the Indian's way, and she would form a bridge between the two cultures that would ultimately help to restore the tribal status of her nation.

Gladys Tantaquidgeon was born on June 15, 1899, near Montville in southeastern Connecticut, the third of the seven living children of Harriet and John Tantaquidgeon. Three other children had died in infancy. Gladys's mother was skilled at the crafts of beading, sewing, and quilting. Although her father was primarily a farmer, he, too, was skilled at native crafts and excelled at wood carving, basket weaving, and stone masonry. The family lived in a rambling farmhouse across the road from an ancient hill that had been a stronghold in the defense of Mohegan lands from intrusion by the Narragansett tribe from the east in the seventeenth century.

Gladys Tantaquidgeon (pronounced Tant-a-QUID'geon, and which means "going along fast on the land or in the water") is a member of the Mohegan, an Algonquin tribe, distantly related to but different from the Mohican tribe of New York State. Around the time of the arrival of English settlers the tribe migrated from New York State to the southeastern part of Connecticut and was originally associated with the neighboring Pequot tribe. Around 1635 a conflict in tribal leadership between the Pequot sachem (chief) Sassacus and his brother-in-law Uncas caused the people to separate into two tribes. Uncas moved with his followers to the west bank of the Thames River and claimed for his people the name Mohegan, meaning "wolf people." In 1637 the Mohegan fought with the English and the Narragansett tribe against the Pequot, and in 1640 and 1675 fought with the English against the Narragansett. Chief Uncas was Gladys Tantaquidgeon's ninth generation grandfather.

Since 1638 the Mohegan tribe has enjoyed cordial diplomatic relations with first the Crown Colony and later with the State of Connecticut, but over the years they watched their reservation shrink as the white man encroached more and more upon their lands. In 1790 the tribe held about 2,700 acres of property. By 1872 the only property left was the church and the tribal burying grounds.

In 1830 the United States government passed the Indian Removal Act, which attempted to force tribes living east of the Mississippi to relinquish their land in exchange for western prairie land. Only those tribes who attended church and provided schooling for their children could avoid such displacement. Thus the Mohegans built a church on their land that also served as a school, named the Indian Congregational Church of Montville, a church that stands to this day. In 1978 the tribe sought formal recognition from the United States government, and it was finally granted in 1994.

Gladys's parents raised her and her siblings in accordance with traditional Indian beliefs. Her mother trimmed her hair only by the waning moon to insure its thickness and health. Her father planted a cedar tree when she was born and taught her to divine for water under ground with forked sticks made of forest woods. Both parents taught their children to respect their Indian heritage, to love the land, and to appreciate the value of hard work. At the same time they were very much aware of the white culture of the twentieth century that was swirling around them just down the road from Mohegan Hill in Uncasville.

Gladys attended the non-Indian local school, and after school she was free to roam with her brothers and sisters through the woods surrounding their house searching for arrowheads—concrete evidence of the presence of their ancestors. In winter the children enjoyed skating parties on the Thames River and raced on homemade sleds. As a youngster Gladys was taught to sew and cook and learned to make quilts and pincushions. She helped her tribe celebrate the Wigwam, or corn festival, in the fall. The Wigwam (which means, "come into my home") featured delicious Indian foods and offered Indian crafts for sale—beaded purses made by the women and carved bowls, spoons, and baskets made by the men. The Wigwam celebration brought the tribal members together and offered Gladys and her family a chance to feel "one with the spirit of all Mohegans."

When Gladys was about eight years old, her parents moved to New London, where she attended Nathan Hale Grammar School for about seven years before the family moved back to Mohegan Hill. Although Gladys never attended high school, she was far from uneducated. She continued to be instructed by the grandmothers in the traditional tribal beliefs. The Nanus taught her that cedar and quartz, sweet grass and corn could evoke good spirits and could protect against bad spirits. She learned the meanings of Mohegan symbols like The Trail of Life symbol, whose arrow points east to west, signifying the passage of spirits and the path

of the sun. The Trail begins in the east with birth, goes on to death
and entrance into the spirit world in the west, and circles back
again to rebirth in the east; the four-domed medallion represents
the four directions. Gladys learned never to gather more herbs than
she needed and which plants were poisonous. But her education
was further enhanced by her close relationship with a young
anthropologist named Frank Speck.

Frank Speck had come as a student to study the tribal language spoken by Gladys's great aunt, Fidelia Fielding, who was a
friend of the Speck family. Fidelia welcomed Frank into her home
in the Connecticut woods, introduced him to the ways of the
Indian, and filled him with a lasting love and respect for the knowledge, traditions, and languages of Native American tribes. Since
Fidelia was the last to speak the language of the Mohegan tribe,
Frank's close relationship with her offered him a unique opportunity to study that dying language and imbued him with a commitment to preserve and record dying languages and cultures
throughout the Native American world.

Frank Speck would go on to become a professor of anthropology at the University of Pennsylvania. He returned often to his
friends on Mohegan Hill and eventually translated four of Fidelia's
diaries. He also enjoyed a lasting friendship with Gladys's older
brother Harold, who later became chief of the tribe. On his visits
to the tribe Frank also struck up a friendship with young Gladys,
and she in turn showed an interest in his work. He and his wife
began to include Gladys on their summer vacations and invited
Gladys and Harold to visit them at their home in New Hampshire.
There the Tantaquidgeons met members of other tribes—the
Penobscot and the Micmac. Through Frank Gladys learned of a
world far beyond the comfortable family compound on Mohegan
Hill. So in 1919, at the age of twenty, Gladys began the study of
anthropology at the University of Pennsylvania, with Frank Speck

as her mentor. In addition to her formal studies, she acted as his assistant and was often sent to visit and research other eastern tribes.

In 1928 Gladys lived with and studied the Gay Head and Mashpee Indians of Massachusetts. Like the Mohegan, the Gay Head and Mashpee believed in the existence of the mythical Granny Squannit, leader of the Makiawisug, or Little People of the forest who, if she wished, could help the tribal medicine man or woman select the right plant to secure a cure for his or her patient. Legend advised that small offerings of food or wine must be left for Granny Squannit in the forest in tiny baskets. The next day the gifts would be gone, and in their place would be the correct herb or plant that would effect the cure the medicine man or woman was seeking. Granny Squannit's husband, Moshup, was also a respected folk hero. Moshup's strength was legend; it was believed he was strong enough to capture whales. Some Indians reported seeing Granny Squannit and Moshup, while others asserted they were invisible.

In 1930 Gladys began studying the Delaware Indians of Oklahoma, specifically their medical practices and folk beliefs. She was aided in this study by a member of the tribe, Wi-tapanóxwe (pronounced Wee-tah-pah-NOKH-way), whose name means "walks with daylight," and whose visit to Philadelphia was sponsored in part by the Pennsylvania Historical Commission. Wi-tapanóxwe—a medicine man himself—reminded Gladys that the Indians had lived healthy lives before the coming of the white settlers and that such health depended on "pure, natural" food which modern-day Indians found difficult to obtain. The Delaware Indian still depended on corn or maize as a staple crop and, like the Mohegan, believed it held nourishment for both the body and spirit. Gladys was always very respectful of the information that Wi-tapanóxwe shared with her, as it was believed that the theories, practices, and beliefs of a medicine man or woman were the personal property of the practitioner, who had been blessed with those skills by the Creator.

Gladys later published her findings on the Delaware in a monograph, *Folk Medicine of the Delaware and Related Algonkian Indians.* Included in the book is valuable information from older members of the community about the Mohegan tribe as well, including a detailed list of plants and herbs used as remedies for various maladies. In her work Gladys advises that tea made from dried yarrow leaves might be used to treat liver and kidney problems and tells us that the fresh leaves of the plantain could be used to draw out snake poison. She goes on to report that yokeag (dried, pulverized corn kernels) is a favorite food of the Mohegans, and its uses are many, including a dependable and totable source of nourishment on long trips.

In 1934 Congress passed the Wheeler-Howard Act, also known as the Indian Reorganization Act, which was an attempt by the federal government to correct years of abuse of the Native Americans, including the practice regarded as "forced assimilation." At the closing of the nineteenth century Indian culture was still considered by the majority of the population to be inferior to that of white, European settlers. Thus, Indians were strongly encouraged by the federal government to turn away from their ancestry, forego their language, and embrace a strictly "American" culture. Indian tribal governments and religions were eradicated. Children were removed from the reservations and sent to distant boarding schools where strict discipline was often imposed and where the ability of their parents to influence their education and upbringing was severely restricted.

Fidelia Fielding had been forbidden to speak her native Mohegan language in such a school and so had been afraid to teach it to Gladys. Indians were discouraged from doing beadwork, weaving, and using religious and ceremonial icons such as dolls and sacred images. They were afraid to teach their children the sacred dances and tribal celebrations.

By 1929 it was acknowledged that the policy of forced assimilation had been a dismal failure, and the Wheeler-Howard Act of 1934 was passed in an attempt to reverse some of that damage. The act encouraged tribes to return to self-government and to re-establish tribal councils and identity. It encouraged the restoration of cultural practices, including knowledge of native languages. Funds were made available to tribes for the establishment of cooperative business enterprises. Schools were re-established on the reservations, and in 1946 a special Indian Claims Commission was established for the express purpose of allowing tribes to make claims for lands taken from them in the past.

In 1934 Gladys was hired by the federal government to assist in administering the benefits of the Wheeler-Howard Act. One of her duties as an employee of the Bureau of Indian Affairs was to determine which young Indians might be eligible to receive educational scholarships under the act, and to this end she traveled throughout New England visiting other tribes.

She was then sent west to South Dakota to work among the Lakota Sioux in an effort to acquaint those tribes with the benefits available to them under the new act. There on a sprinkling of reservations throughout the state Gladys discovered fellow Indians living in abject poverty, confined to lands ill-suited to agriculture, with their individual tribal identities in ruins. She and her co-workers lived among the tribes and shared both their isolation and their deprivations. Winters were harsh, food was scarce, and death often visited even the youngest tribal members. One of Gladys's jobs was to travel the reservations, advising parents that their children would no longer attend boarding schools but would be educated on the reservation. This change created anxiety among the parents, who feared they would be responsible for providing food and clothing for their children all winter. Gladys tried to allay their fears and assure them that the government would provide for their needs. She found her job was a bit easier because she herself was an Indian. "Some of the Sioux were not too keen on having a government agent present," she told an interviewer in later years, "but because of my Indian descent I was accepted."

But she was not always accepted everywhere, and at times she was forced to face the unpleasant realities of racial discrimination. Indians, like blacks, were often asked to sit in the back of a bus and were frequently denied service in restaurants and shops.

After three years of working with the Sioux, Gladys accepted another federal position with the Indian Arts and Crafts Board, which represented an attempt by the government to restore respect for traditional Indian artwork and ceremonies. This job was more suited to Gladys's talents and heritage. Both of her parents were gifted native artists. In addition to her skills in the medical arts, Gladys herself had been taught as a child the traditional arts of basket weaving, beadwork, and sewing. Now she traveled throughout the Dakotas, Montana, and Wyoming, encouraging Indians to again create native crafts and to revive native dances and ceremonies. She assisted them in marketing their crafts and encouraged them to place their work in museums. Respect for Indian art grew and was encouraged by such public figures as First Lady Eleanor Roosevelt.

In 1947, after years of travel and work, Gladys retired from government employment and returned to her home on Mohegan Hill. Her three Nanus had died. Now it was time for her to assume the role of Nanu, to counsel younger tribal members, to continue her work as a medicine woman, and to protect the identity of the Mohegan tribe. In 1931 her father and brother had built the Tantaquidgeon Indian Museum in Uncasville as a home for the artifacts of their tribe. Gladys would now use the experience and knowledge she had learned in her government job to help her brother further develop the Mohegan museum.

After a brief stint as a social worker in a nearby prison, she retired to work exclusively in the museum. Gladys had collected Indian art during her work in the west, and these she also displayed in the family museum. In addition to these artifacts from other tribes, the Tantaquidgeon Indian Museum exhibits items that specifically demonstrate the history of the Mohegan tribe, from the tiny baskets used to offer gifts to the Makiawisug to the larger, more elaborate baskets woven by tribal members. There are arrowheads and tomahawks, mortars and pestles that had been used to grind corn, and birch bark canoes that were used as transportation. As its collections and reputation grew, two more rooms were added, and the museum welcomed visitors from around the world. Today the Tantaquidgeon Indian Museum is open to the public from Memorial Day to Labor Day and is said to be the oldest museum run by Indians in the United States.

For centuries the Mohegan had suffered the indignity of having their burial grounds desecrated, looted of the sacred objects that had been buried with their ancestors. Ancient jewelry, stone pipes, bowls, and arrowheads have found their way over the years into the collections of various museums and historical societies. Gladys and her fellow Mohegans have tried for years to reclaim these items and were encouraged by the passage in 1990 of the Native American Graves Protection and Repatriation Act. The tribe continues to work with museums and historical societies to reclaim those sacred objects that are vital to the history of their tribe.

In addition to working in the museum Gladys assumed responsibility for a cache of tribal papers bequeathed to her care from Nanu Emma Baker—birth certificates, marriage papers, death certificates, and postcards from Mohegans who had traveled around the world. In 1978, when the tribe applied to the federal government for formal recognition of their status as a tribe, the papers that Gladys and Emma Baker collected and preserved offered just the crucial evidence the tribe needed. In an interview in the *New York Times* on June 4, 1997, a historian for the Bureau of Indian Affairs reported that Gladys's tribal archives provided the key to tribal identity. "We needed those pieces of papers," historian Virginia DeMarre declared. "They left no questions whatsoever." Tribal recognition of the Mohegans led to the building of the Mohegan Sun Casino in Uncasville, Connecticut, one of a string of gambling casinos built by Native American tribes over the last few years.

Kudos for Gladys have been many. In 1986 she was honored by the University of Connecticut with an award named for her, in recognition of her role in "diminishing the dual invisibility of women of minority cultures in the United States." In 1992 the Mohegan tribe bestowed upon Gladys official status as medicine woman; in 1993 she was awarded an honorary doctoral degree by the University of Pennsylvania; and on June 15, 1999, a day declared by the State of Connecticut as Gladys Tantaquidgeon Day, she celebrated her one hundredth birthday with a gala celebration replete with honors from many quarters, including representative of other tribes. She never married and, at press time, still lives at her home with her family in Uncasville.

Gladys Tantaquidgeon was born at a time when respect for the Native American was almost nonexistent. Indians were often vilified and stereotyped by whites as violent, naked savages. She has fought against this prejudice her entire life. She left her comfortable family home to travel and work with both cultures in an attempt to administer the white man's laws to her people. It has not always been an easy task. The Indian has traditionally been wary of the white man's promises, with the memory of hundreds of years of abuse still fresh in their minds.

Gladys's life has touched three centuries, and throughout she has labored to keep the spirit of her tribe alive and to instill respect for tribal history in the young Mohegans of today. She has treasured the arts, crafts, and medicinal remedies of her people and has encouraged other tribes to do the same. Where there were no written records, she collected the stories and wrote them down for future generations to learn from and enjoy. And like her brother, Chief Harold Tantaquidgeon, when she told those stories she admonished her fellow Mohegans to, "Listen, and never forget."

She has worked ceaselessly to promote greater understanding of the Mohegans, to preserve her tribe's identity, and to establish its sovereignty for future generations. While she travels her life's trail, she embodies beautifully the Mohegan belief that future generations can be guided by the wisdom of their past.

BIBLIOGRAPHY

ANNA WARNER BAILEY

Burnham, H. E., Rev. *The Battle of Groton Heights: A Story of the Storming of Fort Griswold and the Burning of New London of the 6th of September, 1781.* New London, Conn.: Press of the Day Publishing Co., 1899.

Federal Writers Project, Workers Progress Administration (WPA). *Connecticut American Guide Series: A Guide to Its Roads, Lore, People.* Boston: Houghton Mifflin, 1938.

DePauw, Linda Grant. *Founding Mothers: Women on America in the Revolutionary Era.* Boston: Houghton Mifflin Co., 1975.

Greenblatt, Miriam. *America at War: The War of 1812.* New York: Facts on File, 1994.

Ketcham, Richard M., ed. *The American Heritage Book of the Revolution.* New York: American Heritage Publishing Co., 1958.

Kimball, Carol W. *The Groton Story.* Groton, Conn.: Groton Public Library and Information Center, 1991.

"Memoir of Anna Bailey of Groton, Conn." *New London Weekly Chronicle,* January 22, 1851.

Todd, Charles Burr. *In Olde Connecticut, Being a Record of Quaint, Curious and Romantic Happenings There in Colonie Times and Later.* New York: The Grafton Press, 1906.

JULIA EVELINA SMITH AND ABBY HADASSAH SMITH

Gurko, Miriam. *The Ladies of Seneca Falls.* New York: Schocken Books, 1974.

Hard, Walter. *The Connecticut.* New York: Rinehart & Co., 1947.

Housley, Kathleen L. *The Letter Kills but the Spirit Gives Life.* Glastonbury, Connecticut: The Historical Society of Glastonbury, Connecticut, 1993.

Malone, Dumas, ed. *Dictionary of American Biography.* Vol. XVII. New York: Charles Scribner's Sons, 1935.

Smith, Abby. Smith Papers. The Historical Society of Glastonbury, Connecticut.

Smith, Julia E. *Abby Smith and Her Cows With a Report of the Law Case Decided Contrary to Law.* Hartford, Conn., 1877.

Speare, Elizabeth. "Abby, Julia and the Cows." *American Heritage* VIII, no. 4 (June 1957).

More than Petticoats

PRUDENCE CRANDALL

The American Colonization Society. www.denison.edu/~waite/liberia/history/acs.htm.

Chittenden, Elizabeth F. *Profiles in Black and White: Stories of Men and Women Who Fought Against Slavery.* New York: Charles Scribner, 1973.

Fuller, Edmund. *Prudence Crandall: An Incident of Racism in Nineteenth-Century Connecticut.* Middletown, Conn.: Wesleyan University Press, 1971.

Garrison, William Lloyd, ed. *The Liberator.* 1831–1865.

May, Samuel J. *Some Recollections of Our Antislavery Conflict.* Boston: Fields, Osgood and Co., 1869.

New York Public Library Desk Reference. 2nd ed. New York: New York Public Library and the Stonesong Press, 1993.

Report of the Trial of Miss Prudence Crandall Before the County Court for Windham County, August Term 1833. Brooklyn, Conn.: Unionist Press, 1833.

A Statement of Facts Respecting the School for Colored Females in Canterbury, Connecticut, Together With A Report of the Late Trial of Miss Prudence Crandall. Brooklyn, Conn.: Advertiser Press, 1833.

Strane, Susan. *A Whole Souled Woman: Prudence Crandall and the Education of Black Women.* New York: W.W. Norton and Co., 1990.

Yates, Elizabeth. *Prudence Crandall, Woman of Courage.* Honesdale, Penn.: Boyds Mill Press, 1955.

HARRIET BEECHER STOWE

Faber, Doris. *Love and Rivalry: Three Exceptional Pairs of Sisters.* New York: Viking Press, 1983.

Fritz, Jean. *Harriet Beecher Stowe and the Beecher Preachers.* New York: G. P. Putnam and Sons, 1994.

Hedrick, Joan D. *Harriet Beecher Stowe: A Life.* New York: Oxford University Press, 1994.

James, Edward T., Janet Wilson James, and Paul S. Boyer. *Notable American Women 1607–1950.* Vol. III. Cambridge, Mass.: Harvard University Press, 1971.

Stowe, Edward Charles. *Life of Harriet Beecher Stowe.* Cambridge, Mass.: Houghton, Mifflin and Co., 1889.

BIBLIOGRAPHY

Stowe, Harriet Beecher. *Uncle Tom's Cabin or Life Among the Lowly*. Boston: J. P. Jewett & Co. 1852.

———. *Key to Uncle Tom's Cabin*. Boston: J. P. Jewett, 1863.

Stowe, Lyman Beecher. *Saints, Sinners and Beechers*. New York: Blue Ribbon Books, 1934.

CAROLINE MARIA HEWINS

Canfield, Helen S., and Louise Hovde Mortensen, eds. "Library Pioneer." *The Pen Woman Magazine*, December 1967, reprinted from *Elementary English*.

Danton, Emily Miller, ed. *Pioneering Leaders in Librarianship*. Chicago: American Library Association, 1953.

Hewins, Caroline Maria. "How Library Work With Children Has Grown in Hartford and Connecticut." *Library Journal*, February 1914: 2–9.

———. *A Mid-Century Child and Her Books*. New York: Macmillan Co., 1926.

Jagusch, Sybille Anna. *First Among Equals: Caroline M. Hewins and Anne C. Moore, Foundations of Library Work With Children*. College Park: University of Michigan, 1990.

James, Edward T., Janet Wilson James, and Paul S. Boyer. *Notable American Women 1607–1950*. Vol. II. Cambridge, Mass.: Harvard University Press, 1971.

Lindquist, Jennie D. "Caroline M. Hewins and Books for Children." *The Horn Book*. Vol. XXIX, no. 1 (February 1953).

Warren, S. R., and S. N. Clark, eds. *Public Libraries in the United States of America, Part 1, 1876 Report*. Department of the Interior, Bureau of Education. Washington, D.C.: Government Printing Office, 1876.

Wead, Katherine H. "Caroline M. Hewins, Lover of Children." *Hartford Public Library Bulletin*, April 1947.

Wiegand, Wayne A., and Donald G. Davis, Jr. *Encyclopedia of Library History*. New York and London: Garland Publishing, 1994.

MARTHA MINERVA FRANKLIN

Bacon, Margaret Hope. "Ann Preston: Pioneer Woman Doctor." *Friends Journal* (October 1999). www2.gol.com/users/quakers/ann_preston.htm.

Carnegie, Mary Elizabeth. *The Path We Tread: Blacks in Nursing Worldwide, 1854–1994*. New York: National League for Nursing Press, 1995.

Davis, Althea. *Early Black American Leaders in Nursing*. Sudbury, Mass.: Jones and Bartlett Publishers, 1999.

Garraty, John A., and Mark C. Carnes, eds. *American National Biography*. Vol. 8. New York: Oxford University Press, 1999.

Hine, Darlene Clark. *Black Women in White: Racial Conflict and Cooperation in the Nursing Profession 1890–1950*. Bloomington: Indiana University Press, 1989.

National Association of Colored Graduate Nurses. *National Association of Colored Graduate Nurses Records, 1908–1958*. New York: Shomburg Center for Research in Black Culture.

Smith, Jessie Carney, ed. *Notable Black American Women*. Detroit, Mich.: Gale Research, 1992.

MARY JOBE AKELEY

Akeley, Mary L. Jobe. Unpublished manuscripts, Box 5 Diaries, 1913–1918, Archives of the Mystic River Historical Society, Mystic Connecticut.

———. "My Quest in the Canadian Rockies." *Harper's Magazine*, May 1915.

———. *Carl Akeley's Africa, an Account of the Akeley-Eastman-Pomeroy African Hall Expedition of the American Museum of Natural History*. New York: Dodd, Mead & Co., 1930.

———. "Wildlife Sanctuaries Created in Congo." *The New York Times*, March 15, 1931.

———. *Rumble of a Distant Drum*. New York: Dodd, Mead & Co., 1946.

———. *Congo Eden*. New York: Dodd, Mead & Co., 1950.

Crowther, Dawn-Starr. *Mary L. Jobe Akeley*. Phoenix: Arizona State University, 1989.

Forrester, Izola. "Plucky New York Girl's Dash Alone into The Wilds." *World Magazine*, October 5, 1913.

Garraty, John A. and Mark C. Carnes, eds. *American National Biography*. Vol. 1. New York: Oxford University Press, 1999.

Kimball, Carol W. "Camp Mystic Was a Model for Camping." *The Day*, July 16, 1987.

BIBLIOGRAPHY

Miller, Dorcas. *Adventurous Women*. Boulder, Colo.: Pruett Publishing Co., 2000.

Polk, Milbry, and Mary, Tiegreen. *Women of Discovery*. New York: Random House, 2001.

KATHARINE HOUGHTON HEPBURN

"Birth Control Debate Renewed." *The Literary Digest*, December 14, 1935.

Chesler, Ellen. *Margaret Sanger and the Birth Control Movement in America*. New York: Simon and Schuster, 1992.

Garraty, John A., and Mark C. Carnes, eds. *American National Biography*. Vol. 1. New York: Oxford University Press, 1999.

Garrow, David. *Liberty & Sexuality: The Right to Privacy and the Making of Roe v. Wade*. New York: Macmillan Publishing Company, 1994.

Hepburn, Katharine Houghton. *Me: Stories of My Life*. New York: Alfred A. Knopf, 1991.

Leaming, Barbara. *Katharine Hepburn*. New York: Crown Publishers, 1995.

Nichols, Carole. *Votes and More for Women: Suffrage and After in Connecticut*. New York: Institute for Research and the Haworth Press, 1983.

"Sidelights of the Week." *The New York Times*, January 12, 1936, and March 18, 1951.

Stevens, Doris, and Carol O'Hare, eds. *Jailed for Freedom: American Women Win the Vote*. Troutdale, Ore.: New Sage Press, 1995.

SOPHIE TUCKER

Freedland, Michael. *Sophie: The Sophie Tucker Story*. London: Woburn Press, 1978.

Garraty, John A., and Mark C. Carnes, eds. *American National Biography*. Vol. 21. New York: Oxford University Press, 1999.

Orgill, Roxane. *Shout, Sister, Shout! Ten Girl Singers Who Shaped a Century*. New York: Margaret K. McElderry Books, 2001.

Rothe, Anna, ed. *Current Biography: Who's News and Why*. *1945*. New York: The H. W. Wilson Co., 1945.

Sicherman, Green, and Walker Kantrov, eds. *Notable American Women: The Modern Period*. Cambridge, Mass.: Harvard University Press, 1980.

Tucker, Sophie. *Some of These Days*. Garden City, New York: Doubleday, Doran & Co., 1945.

More than Petticoats

MARGARET FOGARTY RUDKIN

Fetridge, Robert H. "Along the Highways and Byways of Finance" *The New York Times,* December 4, 1949.

Garraty, John A., and Mark C. Carnes, eds. *American National Biography.* Vol. 19. New York: Oxford University Press, 1999.

Moritz, Charles, ed. *Current Biography Yearbook,* 1959. New York: Wilson, 1959.

Mossman, Jennifer. *Reference Library of American Women.* Vol. III. Farmington Hills, Mich.: Gale Research, 1999.

"Mrs. Margaret Rudkin Is Dead; Founder of Pepperidge Farm." *The New York Times,* June 2, 1967.

Rudkin, Margaret. *Pepperidge Farm Cookbook.* New York: Atheneum, 1963.

Sicherman, Green, and Walker Kantrov, eds. *Notable American Women: The Modern Period.* Cambridge, Mass.: Harvard University Press, 1980.

EVA LUTZ BUTLER

Butler, David. Butler Family Web site. www.cromwellbutlers.com.

Butler, Eva Lutz. Personal notes and papers. The Indian & Colonial Research Center, Old Mystic, Connecticut.

Caulkins, Frances Manwaring. *History of New London, Connecticut.* New London, Conn.: Press of the Day Publishing Co., 1895.

Grimes, Ellen. Private recollections, "Eva Butler: Friend and Teacher," 1988. Eva Lutz Butler papers. The Indian & Colonial Research Center, Old Mystic, Connecticut.

Kimball, Carol. *The Mashantucket Pequot Historical Conference.* Paper prepared October 23, 1987. The Indian & Colonial Research Center, Old Mystic, Connecticut.

Vergasson, Helen. Private recollections, "Eva Butler," 1988. Eva Lutz Butler papers. The Indian & Colonial Research Center, Old Mystic, Connecticut.

Zeppieri, Jackie. Personal correspondence with author Antonia Petrash, July 11, 2002.

BIBLIOGRAPHY

GLADYS TANTAQUIDGEON

Fawcett, Melissa Jayne. *The Lasting of the Mohegans, Part I.* Uncasville, Conn.: The Mohegan Tribe, 1995.

————. *Medicine Trail: The Life Lessons of Gladys Tantaquidgeon.* Phoenix: University of Arizona Press, 2000.

Grant, Bruce. *American Indians, Yesterday and Today.* New York: E. P. Dutton & Co., 1958.

Malinowski, Sharon, and Anna Sheets, eds. *The Gale Encyclopedia of Native American Tribes.* Vol. 1. Farmington Hills, Mich.: Gale Research, 1998.

Spencer, Robert F., and Jesse D. Jennings. *The Native Americans.* 2nd ed. New York: Harper & Row, 1977.

Tantaquidgeon, Gladys. *Folk Medicine of the Delaware and Related Algonkian Indians.* Harrisburg, Penn.: Pennsylvania Historical and Museum Commission, 1972.

Voight, Virginia Frances. *Mohegan Chief: The Story of Harold Tantaquidgeon.* New York: Funk & Wagnalls Co., 1965.

INDEX

INDEX

ABOUT THE AUTHOR

Antonia Petrash was born and raised in New York and enjoys a deep and abiding interest in the history of the area, especially the history of its extraordinary women. In addition to her writing career, she works as a librarian and archivist and manages a small local history collection on Long Island. She is also the author of Globe Pequot's *More than Petticoats: Remarkable New York Women.* Antonia resides in Glen Cove, New York.